I0887557

Praise for *A Charge to Keep*

"With *A Charge to Keep* Rev. Taylor offers essential insight and practical knowledge in pastoring in the current climate. With each page I saw options and opportunities I wish I would have taken advantage of as I tackled the same problems. A must read for new pastors."

—Rev. Paul P. Martin, Esq.

"Too often, we separate the secular from the sacred, missing the truth that 'all things work together for good,' which includes the skills we develop in the corporate world. This compartmentalization has weakened our churches, and Pastor Taylor addresses this by showing how all of our skills, including our secular ones, are a starting point that can lead us to greater opportunities for growth. His work challenges the church to move beyond mediocrity by debunking some of the most damaging myths about its organization and administration. A must read for any church leader committed to advancing God's Kingdom in the world."

—Rev. Dr. Hugh B. Marriott

SUPERVISOR, EIGHTH EPISCOPAL DISTRICT AME

"Kevin T. Taylor's *A Charge to Keep* sheds light on the complexities of leadership in both secular and sacred arenas. As a seasoned religious leader, he advocates using one's professional expertise in navigating the challenges faced in church leadership. The principles he shares are practical and replicable. It is a much needed resource."

—Rev. Dr. Faye Banks Taylor

PASTOR, ST. MARK'S CHAPEL AME CHURCH, KINGSTON, NY

PRESIDING ELDER, ALBANY-KINGSTON DISTRICT, AME CHURCH

ASSISTANT PROFESSOR, NEW BRUNSWICK THEOLOGICAL SEMINARY, NEW BRUNSWICK, NJ

"*A Charge to Keep* by Kevin T. Taylor is a must read for any leader seeking clear, actionable strategies to navigate tough decisions with integrity. Taylor's unique background as a nonprofit CEO and church pastor provides a fresh perspective, blending practical leadership tools with relatable storytelling. Whether you're turning around an organization or balancing life and work, this book offers valuable insights applicable across sectors. Highly recommend!"

—Analiza Quiroz Wolf

CEO AND FOUNDER, WOMEN OF COLOR RISE

AUTHOR, *THE MYTHS OF SUCCESS: A WOMAN OF COLOR'S GUIDE TO LEADERSHIP; NATIVE AMERICANS WHO INSPIRE US; LATIN AMERICANS WHO INSPIRE US; ASIAN AMERICANS WHO INSPIRE US; BALIKBAYAN: A FILIPINO HOMECOMING*

"Kevin T. Taylor nails the critical gaps between the church and businesses. *A Charge to Keep* will have you positively rethinking your relationship with both entities and challenging the status quo. As a business CEO, Kevin's book affirms the importance of making room for employees to 'bring their whole selves' to work as they pursue their careers. *A Charge to Keep* is a must read for all."

—Brenda J. Curry

CEO, CURTOM BUILDING AND DEVELOPMENT CORPORATION

PARTNER, CURTOM-DUNSMUIR

"The startup community is overflowing with incredibly talented entrepreneurs with outstanding ideas, many of whom have never managed people nor navigated the uncharted waters necessary to scale their businesses. *A Charge to Keep* provides practical leadership examples—and field-tested, proven practices—to get results. Whether you are a novice leader or a seasoned professional, this book belongs in your library and is a worthy investment."

—Juliana Garaizar

FOUNDING PARTNER, ENERGY TECH NEXUS

GENERAL PARTNER, PORTFOLIA RISING AMERICA

GENERAL PARTNER, MALAIKA VENTURES

VENTURE PARTNER, CLIMATETECH GLOBAL VENTURES

KAUFFMAN FELLOW

VC INCLUDE FELLOW

a Charge *to* Keep

REV. KEVIN T. TAYLOR

a Charge *to* Keep

IMMUTABLE LEADERSHIP LESSONS FROM THE **C-SUITE** TO THE **PULPIT**

Advantage | Books

Published by Advantage Books, Charleston, South Carolina.
An imprint of Advantage Media.

Printed in the United States of America.

10 9 8 7 6 5 4 3 2 1

ISBN: 979-8-89188-007-8 (Paperback)
ISBN: 979-8-89188-008-5 (eBook)

Library of Congress Control Number: 2025914655

Cover design by Analisa Smith.
Layout design by Lance Buckley.

Advantage Books is an imprint of Advantage Media Group. Advantage Media helps busy entrepreneurs, CEOs, and leaders write and publish a book to grow their business and become the authority in their field. Advantage authors comprise an exclusive community of industry professionals, idea-makers, and thought leaders. For more information go to **advantagemedia.com**.

07-18-2025 10:22

To Emily

Thank you for walking beside me on this journey. Whether from the highest mountain or the lowest valley, the view is always better with you.

To My Children

Daddy loves you! Always remember, in the words of Dr. Maya Angelou, "You are the dream and hope of the slave."

CONTENTS

FOREWORD

Finally, a leadership approach that doesn't force you to choose between biblical wisdom and organizational effectiveness. This isn't just another leadership book—it's a practical framework that has delivered measurable improvements in staff retention, decision-making efficiency, and organizational performance. In today's high-pressure business environment, where burnout plagues executives and companies struggle to maintain excellence and retain purpose-driven talent, *A Charge to Keep* arrives at this critical moment with proven innovative solutions that transcend traditional boundaries between faith and commerce.

The title, inspired by Charles Wesley's timeless hymn and Leviticus 8:35, speaks to leaders who stand at the intersection of spiritual wisdom and organizational stewardship. Just as ancient leaders maintained their sacred duty at the entrance of the tent of meeting, today's leaders face a similar calling—to build organizations that achieve immediate impact and eternal significance.

Kevin T. Taylor writes from this intersection with unique authority. As a successful chief executive officer, educator, and pastor, he developed concrete tools and frameworks that have proven successful in complex business environments while maintaining spiritual integrity. His approach isn't theoretical—it demonstrates how spiritual principles and sound business practices create sustainable, mission-driven growth.

The results validate his methodology. Through Taylor's principles, ChaplainCare is forging a new generation of leaders who integrate spiritual wisdom with business acumen seamlessly. ROI metrics tell the story: stronger teams, enhanced decision-making, and improved bottom-line results—all while deepening mission impact.

A struggling urban ministry magnified its impact tenfold using these principles. Similarly, a corporate educational institution achieved dramatic improvements in engagement, retention, and academic outcomes.

Taylor's Recommendation Chart is at the heart of these transformations, helping organizations navigate complex decisions from multimillion-dollar acquisitions to culture change initiatives. Leaders consistently report accelerated decision-making, stronger buy-in, and more effective implementation. Through practical case studies and Scripture-based methodologies, Taylor shows how to:

- Cultivate organizational cultures that inspire extraordinary performance and purpose
- Transform abstract vision statements into measurable impact
- Create sustainable growth through values-based leadership
- Develop future leaders who integrate spiritual wisdom with organizational stewardship
- Align operational excellence with eternal purpose

For skeptics who question whether faith and business truly mix, *A Charge to Keep* offers real-world evidence and rigorous methodology. For religious leaders seeking operational excellence without compromising values, Taylor demonstrates how biblical wisdom coupled with sound management amplifies rather than dilutes mission impact—much like Joseph's divine wisdom enabled Egypt's organizational success. This isn't about imposing faith on business or reducing faith to metrics—it's about unleashing the full potential of both.

Your investment in this transformative work extends beyond professional development—proceeds support nonprofit organizations focused on transforming lives, developing next- generation leaders, and strengthening communities through evidence-based lifelong learning programs. In an era demanding performance excellence and eternal significance, *A Charge to Keep* provides your road map to building an organization that thrives in immediate impact and lasting purpose.

Reverend (Dr.) Johnny Poole

FOUNDER, CEO, CHAPLAINCARE LLC

INTRODUCTION

"Don't mix religion and business."

I've heard variations of this phrase my entire life, from both inside the church and inside business circles. Business leaders say, "If you want to go to church, that's fine. Just keep your beliefs to yourself."

Church leaders who aren't otherwise criticizing the need to be bivocational say, "Your nine-to-five job is great, but don't try to bring your business principles to a religious establishment."

But here is the reality. In America today, workers want purpose in their jobs, and churches need strong business leaders. Let's start with the first part of that sentence. A 2024 Deloitte study revealed that "nearly all Gen Zs and millennials want purpose-driven work, and they are not afraid to turn down work that doesn't align with their values. Having a sense of purpose is key to workplace satisfaction and well-being."[1]

This same study found that 86 percent of Gen Z and 89 percent of millennials "say having a sense of purpose is very or somewhat important to their overall job satisfaction and well-being."[2] Also, nearly half of Gen Z and millennial workers "have rejected an assignment or project based

1 Deloitte, *2024 Gen Z and Millennial Survey: Living and Working with Purpose in a Transforming World*, accessed October 28, 2024, https://www.deloitte.com/global/en/issues/work/content/genz-millennialsurvey.html.

2 Deloitte, *2024 Survey*.

on their personal beliefs" or "have turned down an employer based on their personal ethics or beliefs."[3] Thus, businesses that don't make room for their employees to bring their whole selves to the table might miss out on a large percentage of qualified candidates.

On a different but related note, churches in America are in trouble today, with many closing their doors. While the reasons for this are numerous, James Harnsberger of Faithful Steward writes that one of the primary reasons is financial mismanagement. Harnsberger notes, "Many churches have failed to adapt to the changing economic landscape and have not implemented sound financial practices. In some cases, churches have overextended themselves by taking on large building projects or other financial commitments without securing the necessary funding or ensuring long-term sustainability."[4]

A study conducted by the Presbyterian Foundation found that the lack of solid business practices in the church is devastating. In fact, "only 10% of churches experiencing financial fraud report it, and when they do, the average amount is $70,000. One-third of churches will suffer some form of financial misconduct. It is estimated that, worldwide by 2025, churches and nonprofit organizations will lose $90 billion to fraud."[5] This is a reality even in my own AME denomination after it was recently revealed that over $100 million in retirement funds went missing.[6]

---

3 Deloitte, *2024 Survey*.

4 James Harnsberger, "The Growing Number of Failing Churches in the United States," Faithful Steward, February 1, 2024, https://faithfulsteward.co/the-growing-number-of-failing-churches-in-the-united-states/.

5 Chuck Toney, "Sound Financial Practices Are Key to Good Stewardship in Churches," Presbyterian Foundation, October 9, 2023, https://www.presbyterianfoundation.org/resources/news/sound-financial-practices-are-key-to-good-stewardship-in-churches/.

6 Leonardo Blair, "AME Church Will No Longer Allow 'One Person to Count the Money' after Nearly $100M Goes Missing," *Christian Post*, March 25, 2022, https://www.christianpost.com/news/ame-church-sued-after-100m-goes-missing.html.

Clearly, good business leaders have something to learn from good faith-based leaders. And good faith-based leaders have something to learn from the business community. If, as an employer, you say to employees, "Leave your faith at home," you've ignored a large part of their being and set your organization up for failure. If, as a church leader, you say to parishioners, "Leave your business skills at home," you miss out on the unique giftings of people who represent one more part of the body of Christ.

As 2 Corinthians 5:7 says, we walk by "faith and not by sight." In a religious context, this means that our steps are ordered by God, and even if we cannot see the steps ahead of us, we move forward anyway with the faith that where God leads us is where we need to be. People of faith bring the same sense of assurance to their workplaces, particularly during challenging times when the road ahead may appear dark or less traveled. Leaders of faith can play an important role in keeping key constituents motivated and engaged. They are often culture champions for an organization or the resident CEO: chief *encouragement* officer.

From the church's perspective, my financial acumen has opened many doors for me. To paraphrase Proverbs 18:16, "Your gifts will make room for you," and I can attest that my gifts have indeed made room for me. When one of the churches I pastored faced foreclosure, my business background helped me step in and help the congregation refinance its mortgage, saving them three percentage points in interest. This intervention stabilized the church and allowed it to thrive today.

I consider myself a change agent, and I can help move communities from a place of crisis to where God is calling them to be. This ability to transform has been a hallmark of my ministry. I've gone to churches in need and helped turn them around, placing them on more solid footing financially and spiritually. While I may not have stayed at these churches long enough to taste the fruit from the trees I've planted, I can look back and see that the fruit the congregation now tastes is partly a result of the hard work I invested in tilling the soil.

On the professional side, I have similarly applied my skills to help change organizations experiencing identity crises or founder's dilemmas, or those needing process improvement and efficiency. I've used my experience as a visionary pastor to help move these businesses closer to fulfilling their missions. As a result, my financial acumen has propelled me from roles like interim executive director or COO to positions such as CFO and CEO across multiple types of organizations and industries.

The beauty of working in church and business communities is that it's fundamentally changed the way I live in every facet of life. Looking back, I'm convinced one of the primary reasons I thrived in certain settings and failed in others was that I brought my full self to the table. I find it interesting that leaders often talk about the importance of being their true and authentic selves. Yet, in practice, they often deny parts of themselves because they feel that certain aspects of their identity must remain hidden to achieve success.

If they're in church, they hide their business acumen. If they're in business, they hide their faith-based values that could empower those in their organization to find a more lasting purpose in what they do. As a result, they fail to see that the lessons they acquire in one area of life can be incredibly beneficial in another.

This is a mindset I'm hoping to change. I'm a much stronger pastor because I've participated in numerous high-quality professional development sessions at work. I understand the importance of crafting a strong budget, leading meetings well, presenting complicated information in palatable ways, and valuing people's time, and I bring that same skill set to the church.

I'm also a much stronger business leader because, as a pastor, I've developed greater empathy for others. For example, I recently read Mohammad Anwar's book *Love as a Business Strategy.* It's a fantastic read that discusses how businesses can grow by fostering empathy among team members. It talks about making people feel valued during the interview process—inviting them in, being transparent, and making them feel like part of the organization from the start. In it, Anwar writes that "love as a business strategy means putting people at the center of work by creating a workplace that puts humanity first."[7]

Because I believe in the value of humanity, everyone at church receives about ten cards from me each year. These include birthdays, anniversaries, and holidays. If someone gets sick or experiences a family loss, a card is coming their way. This practice also extends to work; there's always something for every holiday. These principles are integral to who I am.

I understand if you have held these two worlds of business and faith as far apart as possible. But I hope that the following pages challenge you to rethink your position. If you're a business leader, consider what your workforce could look like if you encouraged your employees to bring their whole selves to the table. This doesn't mean you allow endless proselytizing, but it means that you make a meaningful effort to tap into your team members' true motivations. You don't just hire people to fulfill a job; you hire them for a job that helps them achieve their higher purpose.

If you're a church leader, consider what your congregation could look like if you encouraged each person to bring the full depth and breadth of their wisdom to the table. Instead of feeling intimidated

---

7 Mohammad F. Anwar, Frank E. Danna, Jeffrey F. Ma, and Christopher J. Pitre, *Love as a Business Strategy: Resilience, Belonging & Success* (Lioncrest Publishing, 2021), 24, Kindle.

by those with solid workforce talents, you invited them to be part of your inner circle.

Regardless of which perspective you find yourself in today, this book aims to help you build a financially sound, relationally strong, and courageously scalable organization. I'm not an expert, but I can be your guide. I can't promise a straight line of success, but I can show you common pitfalls to avoid and tips I've learned along the way.

The twelve principles I share in this book are like tools in a toolbox. The reason most homes have a toolbox in the garage is that homeowners never know when they'll need an Allen wrench, hammer, or screwdriver. But when they do, they'll have the tools on hand to handle whatever challenges they face. Similarly, it's unlikely you'll need all twelve tools I offer at this present moment. But if you're in leadership long enough, rest assured you will. And when you do, I want you to be ready.

Adopting new tools means having the willingness to change. In the following chapters, I will describe two case studies—one from my church experience and the other from the boardroom. Some approaches come from church leaders, while others come from executives. However, regardless of whether you are a leader in a C-suite company, a church, or any other for-profit or nonprofit institution, these twelve principles will still apply.

They are my non-negotiables and have served me very well. And I'm confident that if you follow them, they will do the same for you.

PRINCIPLE 1

Strong Financial Leadership Is the Foundation for Every Great Organization

Financial success is not a hard science. It's a soft skill, where how you behave is more important than what you know.

—MORGAN HOUSEL

Strong financial leadership is the common denominator between successful businesses, churches, and nonprofits. Without it, *no* organization can last.

In theory, every leader knows this, but many underestimate how important this foundation is. I've seen this play out in churches, businesses, and nonprofits. Through their words, leaders will talk about how important finances are, but through their actions, they will live as though they're an afterthought.

As someone who has stepped into numerous leadership roles, I ensure that one of the first steps I take whenever I work with a new organization is to do a rigorous financial analysis. When I do this, I almost always find that the real financial truth is not as it initially appeared. It's usually a lot worse.

In an article titled "Five Top Causes of Business Bankruptcy and How to Avoid Them," Stephen Nalley of *Kiplinger Personal Finance* notes that "poor financial management is one of the most prevalent reasons companies go bankrupt."[8] Through personal experience, I've witnessed firsthand that the primary reason organizations meet their demise is due to financial crises. Take the charter school space, for example. What typically brings these schools down isn't weak academic performance but financial difficulties that weren't adequately addressed.

This is why it's imperative to grasp your company's financial situation sooner rather than later. Understanding your organization's finances allows you to identify potential challenges before they become insurmountable problems. Regardless of whether you're a new or established leader, it's critical that you know your financial runway and how long your organization can operate before it needs additional funding.

By proactively managing finances, you can steer your organization toward stability and growth rather than reacting to crises as they arise. For example, in 2012, the Union African Methodist Episcopal (AME) Church in Warwick, New York, faced a financial crisis. Weeks before my assignment, the church leaders had borrowed $50,000 from the denomination to keep the church from being sold in foreclosure, and repaying the existing debt was a challenge.

To continue staving off foreclosure, they needed to refinance. After asking several other ministers to take on the job and being rejected, the bishop turned to me. As an experienced corporate financial manager, I was confident I was qualified to step into the

8 Stephen Nalley, "Five Top Causes of Business Bankruptcy and How to Avoid Them," *Kiplinger Personal Finance*, July 9, 2024, https://www.kiplinger.com/kiplinger-advisor-collective/top-causes-of-business-bankruptcy-and-how-to-avoid-them.

role, and in the fall of that year, the bishop assigned me to become Union's lead pastor.

Beyond saving souls and helping the church become viable in the future, my first priority was maneuvering the church out of its unstable financial dilemma. This started with negotiating a loan refinancing with a bank. The timeline was tight, and I had around four months to seal the deal and financially stabilize the church.

In most corporate situations, refinancing a $300,000 construction loan converted to a traditional mortgage at 9 percent was certainly doable. But this situation was especially tough. The church had established some poor financial habits, and they needed a change agent to step in and turn things around.

THREE CRITICAL STEPS

Stepping into this role, I realized there were three critical steps I had to take. These steps are ones I'd recommend any leader take if they're faced with a similar financially challenging situation. The first one was obvious.

STEP 1: CONDUCT A DISCOVERY PROCESS

Before making any changes, I had to uncover the facts and see what was behind the problem. I needed to uncover how the church had gotten into this predicament and why it needed the $50,000 bailout in the first place. It did not take long to find some answers.

For starters, the Union church leaders did not routinely pay the bills on time—the $3,600 mortgage payment being at the top of the list. I also learned that the church did not keep records of critical financial data. Since banks require their refinance clients to provide three years of financial data, to say nothing of the loan's annual financial reporting covenant, this would be a problem.

While conducting a discovery process can feel time consuming, I assure you it's necessary and will save you a lot of time, energy, and resources in the long run. If you're new to a business that has run into some financial challenges, the first step you need to take is a full diagnostic.

STEP 2: ESTABLISH TRUST

After I realized where the church was and what needed to be done, the next step was to develop a relationship of trust with the church leaders and congregation. Of course, as in just about any case when a new leader comes in, there was some skepticism about me. Union's leaders were a proud group, and they were embarrassed that a new pastor had been assigned so abruptly to fix their problematic situation.

Recognizing this potential for pushback, I took an unusual but crucial step and immediately reduced my salary by 50 percent. I know this isn't always possible for everyone, but by taking less than the previous pastor, I freed up resources the church could invest in paying bills and keeping up mortgage payments. While that was a personal sacrifice, it helped build trust between me and the parishioners. With this sacrifice and the tithes and offerings that came from my day job in addition to the tithes from my church salary, they could see I was sincere in my mission to get the church on solid financial ground.

As Stephen Covey writes, "The first job of a leader—at work or at home—is to inspire trust. It's to bring out the best in people by entrusting them with meaningful stewardships, and to create an environment in which high-trust interaction inspires creativity and possibility."[9] Overlooking this step makes it ten times harder to move forward.

---

9 Stephen Covey, *The Speed of Trust: The One Thing That Changes Everything.*

STEP 3: DEMONSTRATE COMMITMENT

Above all, I knew I must prioritize the spiritual needs of the congregation and the community. For example, Warwick is in Orange County, a suburb of New York City. Though the school system is solid, the lack of employment opportunities leads to higher incidences of drug use and abuse, teenage pregnancies, and socioeconomic struggles for residents. When I considered the shame that came from the church's financial situation and the fact that Union was one of the few Black churches in the county, I became more committed to the community and increased my involvement in the church. I even volunteered to move into the parsonage adjacent to the church as another sign of my willingness to be their pastor, not just their hired help.

In the years since the new church had been constructed, no pastor had lived in the parsonage full time. That all-in involvement demonstrated I was willing to make sacrifices financially and be a part of the community. They realized I wouldn't be there one day and gone the next. I was committed.

Actions always speak louder than words. As Ralph Waldo Emerson said, "What you are stands over you the while, and thunders so that I cannot hear what you say to the contrary."[10] A popular modern paraphrase says, "What you do speaks so loudly that what you say I don't hear." Words are good, but actions are even more important.

A $6,000 MIRACLE

After I had taken these three steps, the key was to remain focused on the objective. Now that I thoroughly understood the church's financial situation and had built a strong rapport with the parishioners, I was

10 Ralph Waldo Emerson, *Letters and Social Aims*, 1976.

ready to develop and implement a plan to refinance the loan. While the process was routine, it was not without obstacles.

One significant hurdle arose when the bank holding the existing loan informed us that they did not consider the church a stable client and wished to cease working with us entirely. When I approached other banks and hard lenders, they also declined to engage upon learning that the church was in foreclosure status.

The foreclosure was like an albatross around the church's neck, deterring potential lenders. The bank suggested that demonstrating twenty-four months of solid loan payments would position us for the much-needed refinancing. However, we encountered another challenge. To proceed with refinancing, the church was required to submit three years of bank statements and other financial records, which, as noted earlier, we had not maintained.

We contacted a certified accountant to compile these reports, but his fee was $4,000—money we did not have. This forced church members to scramble to locate the necessary data, retrieving bank statements from shoeboxes and other storage places. But it was here I noticed the hand of God at work.

During one of our women's season events, the church hosted a prayer breakfast where I delivered the keynote address on the power and methods of prayer. I emphasized our need to trust in God's ability to meet our needs, including the financial support to help the church overcome its challenges. After the event, a woman I had never met approached me and inquired about the amount needed to resolve our situation. She mentioned that she had recently received a settlement from an accident and wished to tithe a portion to the church.

Reaching into her purse, she later presented me with a check for $6,000, which was more than enough to cover the accountant's fee for preparing the required reports. I was shocked. All I did was simply state our needs without any expectation that someone would provide such a substantial contribution. I certainly would not have imagined a stranger would be the answer to my prayer.

Buoyed by this momentum and the belief that God was still working miracles, the church pressed forward. We began making on-time monthly payments, which we celebrated during offering time each month. As part of our worship, we announced how many consecutive months we had paid the mortgage. This practice not only rallied the congregation around our goal but also strengthened the church's commitment to becoming a financially responsible institution.

Soon, the bank took notice of our efforts to become more reliable. When they learned I was the finance director for a charter school network, they were pleased to know that the church's pastor possessed financial expertise, and I was more encouraged than ever. But then, everything seemed to fall apart.

THE POWER OF FOCUS

In the spring of 2014, much to our surprise, the bank informed our church they were ready to call the loan despite our several months of on-time payments. I was flabbergasted. We had made every payment on time since my arrival and were nowhere near securing another lender. I offered to send them our annual financial statements for review. Although our broker advised against it, I sent them anyway.

The next day, the bank responded with news that made us rejoice. Not only were they willing to keep the loan, but they also offered to reduce the interest rate by three percentage points—from 9 percent to 6 percent. This reduction would decrease our monthly mortgage payment by $600, lowering it from $3,600 to less than $3,000.

They pledged to work with us to restructure the mortgage. However, there was a catch: we needed to come up with more than $18,000 in closing costs in less than six weeks! While this felt impossible, we recognized this as the best path forward. I told the church leaders that we would have to proceed and put our trust in God to provide. There wasn't time to design a new stewardship model or add a major fundraiser to the calendar; we had to rely on our existing plans and faith.

Several days later, I explained our situation to the congregation. Before the meeting concluded, over $3,000 in contributions were on the table toward meeting our goal. Additional tithes and offerings gradually brought us closer to raising the $18,000 required. While we still fell a bit short of the time frame, the bank worked with us, and we hit our goal.

The key takeaway from this experience was the power of focus. Because our church had committed to good habits and was laser focused on our end goal, I believe we experienced the favor of God. One of my favorite passages of scripture that speaks to the power of focus is Hebrews 12:2, which says of Jesus, "For the joy set before him he endured the cross, scorning its shame, and sat down at the right hand of the throne of God."[11] Despite enormous pain and suffering, Jesus stayed focused on his mission, and he expects his followers to do the same.

In September 2014, Union AME Church successfully refinanced its mortgage. With the savings from the reduced mortgage payments and our financial affairs in order, the church increased my salary from $200 to $350 monthly, and we were on much more solid ground. A church that was once considered radioactive had become a place

11 All scripture citations are in the New International Version translation.

where people wanted to be, where ministry was thriving, and where success stories were still being written.

Looking back, I see that my Union assignment gave me some invaluable leadership lessons that profoundly shaped my ministry.

FOUR IMPORTANT LESSONS

The first lesson I learned was the importance of honoring my commitments. As an AME minister, during my ordination process, I committed to go wherever the bishop of our Episcopal district assigned me. Ministers believe such appointments are divinely inspired, and so we trust the godly wisdom of the bishop to match congregations with pastors and ministers with a shepherd's heart.

Pastoring was not just a personal decision. It was a collective choice to work in harmony with others and with God to do something great. Pastoring at Union was an act of faith on the part of the congregation, the bishop, and me. Because I was willing to go to a church that was struggling, I believe God honored my commitment to serve wholeheartedly regardless of the situation.

The second lesson was the power of humility. Philippians 2:3 says, "Do nothing out of selfish ambition or vain conceit. Rather, in humility, value others above yourselves." By taking a pay cut to join this congregation, I'm convinced this was an act of humility that God blessed. Not only did I demonstrate solidarity with the church members, but I believe I aligned my heart with God's heart.

A third lesson was the significance of community. When I moved into the church parsonage to become an integral part of the community, this changed everything. Living among the congregation allowed me to build deeper relationships and better understand their needs and aspirations.

The final lesson was the joy of seeing takers shift into becoming givers. Little by little, I saw our congregation change from having a mindset that said others would bail us out, to being wise stewards of what God had entrusted us to use. We moved from being takers to being givers. In doing so, we followed in the footsteps of a god who, as John 3:16 says, "so loved the world that he *gave* his one and only Son, that whoever believes in him shall not perish but have eternal life."

Regardless of where you are, these lessons will work for you as well. If you honor God in your decision-making, seek to be humble, live in community, and teach those on your team to be givers, you live out the characteristics of the life that God blesses.

This brings me to my second story, which involves the corporate side of leadership.

LEADERSHIP LESSONS:

1. Honor your commitments.
2. Embrace the power of humility.
3. Acknowledge the significance of community.
4. Shift from a spirit of taking to a spirit of giving.

CEO OF FREDERICK DOUGLASS

In July 2018, I stepped into the role of CEO at Frederick Douglass, one of the original fourteen charter public schools in Massachusetts. At the time, we had three campuses: one in New Bedford and two in Boston's Roxbury neighborhood. Right from the start, Frederick Douglass was facing a myriad of challenges, including dropping student numbers, lower donations, and the recent unionization of our staff.

Early on, I spotted a key financial opportunity. The Frederick Douglass Foundation, our fundraising arm, had nearly $2 million sitting in assets. It was like having a rainy-day fund during a financial storm. With enrollment slipping and donations drying up, I pushed to use these funds to invest directly in our students and families.

At the same time, the unionization of our staff added another layer of complexity. Back in March 2018, the previous administration tried to prevent unionization by giving teachers a 4 percent raise and keeping all roles intact. While the union accepted the raise, they kept pushing their organizing efforts.

By February 2019, our senior director of finance reported fewer lottery applications and higher student attrition rates than usual. I flagged this to the board as a warning sign and suggested we right-size the organization to match our enrollment numbers. Despite pushback from the union and some board members who wanted to boost marketing instead, we went ahead with necessary layoffs in the spring. I made it clear that we needed to live within our means to stay afloat.

Amid these staffing issues, we were in regular talks with Boston Private, our main lender, about our financial plans. We knew we'd miss a debt covenant because of the investments we needed to make, so we asked for a waiver and were assured our Boston Private relationship manager was on board. But on October 31, the day before our audit was due to our charter authorizer, the bank pulled the rug out from under us. They said they never committed to a waiver and gave us only two choices: submit the audit late or agree to a forbearance agreement. It was a huge surprise and a tough spot to be in.

Adding to our woes, Frederick Douglass's renewal of its flagship charter school in Roxbury was coming up. The authorizer ended up putting our New Bedford campus on probation due to poor academic performance, which made our turnaround efforts even more urgent. In response, we invested in key roles and academic supports and upgraded our facilities. These moves stretched our finances further and led us to right-size the staff of all three campuses.

The union wasn't happy about the staff cuts, but after a lot of back-and-forth, we got the board to approve of the layoffs despite the negative feedback and the additional enrollment challenges caused by some teachers leaving. Our shaky financial situation and the strict terms of the forbearance agreement also strained our relationship with Boston Private, so we had to negotiate hard to stabilize things. A turning point came when a former board chair and key donor who had stopped supporting us stepped in to help. With his support, we were able to smooth things over with the bank and move forward with our rightsizing plan.

By December 2021, we had hit some major milestones: our charter was renewed with mostly academic conditions, and we closed the New Bedford campus, merged the Roxbury locations, and secured a streamlined contract with Massachusetts's oldest teachers' union. These steps brought us back to a solid financial footing, lifted us out of forbearance with Boston Private, and kept our charter autonomy and fair salary scales intact. Thanks to these efforts, Frederick Douglass was in a much stronger position when the COVID-19 pandemic hit, allowing us to weather the storm better than we might have otherwise.

Throughout this journey, I focused on change-management and continuous improvement, setting up a solid framework for future leaders. When I left Frederick Douglass in December 2021, my second-in-command—and rival in the CEO search process—took over as executive director, and I felt confident moving on to new challenges, knowing that we had built a resilient and stable organization.

REMEMBER: STRONG FINANCIAL LEADERSHIP IS THE FOUNDATION FOR EVERY GREAT ORGANIZATION

Through my time at Union AME Church and Frederick Douglass, I witnessed firsthand how strong financial leadership can kill or save an organization. Leadership is everything. As Tod Bolsinger writes, "Leadership is energizing a community of people toward their own transformation in order to accomplish a shared mission in the face of a changing world."[12]

Sometimes this results in lasting change; other times it does not. For example, today, Union remains a thriving church while Frederick Douglass has fallen on tough times and is shutting its doors for good in 2025. Regardless, in both situations I knew I did the best I could and controlled what only I could control.

Success also looks very different in every situation. Sometimes, success involves an incredible turnaround or rapid expansion. Other times, it means survival. Sometimes, you run your leg of the race, and another leader comes alongside you to carry the baton forward after you step aside. Other times, you run and don't see the results you anticipate. That's OK. The key is to remain committed to your principles.

Building a strong financial foundation for your organization takes time, intentionality, and focus. It's far from easy, but it's wonderfully rewarding.

---

12 Tod E. Bolsinger, *Canoeing the Mountains: Christian Leadership in Uncharted Territory* (InterVarsity Press, 2018), 42.

BULLETIN NOTES

KEY TAKEAWAYS:

- ☑ Strong financial leadership is crucial for any organization's survival and success, yet many leaders underestimate its foundational importance.
- ☑ Leaders facing financial challenges should conduct a thorough discovery process, establish trust with stakeholders, and demonstrate commitment to the organization's mission.
- ☑ Maintaining focus on objectives and cultivating good financial habits can lead organizations to overcome obstacles and achieve financial stability.
- ☑ Key lessons include honoring commitments, embracing humility, valuing community engagement, and encouraging a shift from a taking mindset to a giving one among team members.

KEY QUESTIONS:

1. What are the three critical steps the author recommends leaders take when facing a financially challenging situation? How are these applicable to your organization?
2. How did personal sacrifices contribute to building trust and achieving financial stability in the author's experiences? What sacrifices have you made or are willing to make for the health of your organization?
3. What leadership lessons did the author learn from turning around financially troubled organizations, and how can they be applied elsewhere?

PRINCIPLE 2

The Best Decisions Are Always Made in Proper Context

For me context is the key—from that comes the understanding of everything.

—KENNETH NOLAND

One of the most popular sayings in pastoral circles is "context is king."

Without context, it's impossible to know where you are and where you need to go. Context provides the background and circumstances that give meaning to information or events. Without context, facts or statements can be misunderstood or misinterpreted, leading to confusion and errors in judgment.

The late author and pastor Timothy Keller wrote, "Everyone contextualizes—but few think much about how they are doing it."[13] We contextualize when we wake up and observe our surroundings. We contextualize when we're driving to work and account for the speed limit, weather conditions, and proximity to other cars on the highway.

13 Timothy Keller, *Center Church: Doing Balanced, Gospel-Centered Ministry in Your City* (Grand Rapids, MI: Zondervan, 2012), 97.

We contextualize when we interact with friends based on previous interactions we've had with them.

The need for contextualization is especially relevant in preaching. As a pastor who has preached hundreds of sermons, I know that context is the key to a good message. If I'm speaking from Luke 2 on the story of Christ's birth, I want my listeners to understand the setting.

Why did Mary and Joseph have to travel to Bethlehem? Why would the angel appear to shepherds and not the religious leaders? What was it like to be a shepherd? How did the political culture of that time dictate people's lives?

Answering these questions is what pastors call good exegesis. *Exegesis* involves drawing out the original meaning of the text based on its context, language, and intent. It's an objective approach that aims to uncover what the author intended to communicate. This often requires a deep understanding of historical, cultural, and linguistic factors to interpret the text accurately.

Eisegesis, on the other hand, occurs when the reader imposes their own views, biases, or ideas on the text. Instead of seeking the author's original meaning, eisegesis leads to a subjective interpretation shaped by the reader's perspective, potentially distorting the text's intended message. Exegesis is text-centered and objective, while eisegesis is reader centered and subjective. Exegesis is focused on context, and eisegesis is focused on personal opinion.

Early in my ministry, I had my share of eisegesis moments. Part of this was because my background wasn't rooted in literature or theology. It was rooted in mathematical reasoning and a desire for applause lines and not an application to personal lives. My grade school and postsecondary education shaped my approach to problem-solving and understanding the practical application of theories, whether in politics or scripture. While this approach has its benefits, it also has its downside in interpreting scripture accurately.

In college at Tuskegee University, when I was a youth minister in training, I was asked by my senior pastor to preach for Thanksgiving. Not sure which direction I should go, I stumbled upon a brilliant idea to center the sermon around the meal aspect of Thanksgiving rather than the actual theme of gratitude. I titled my sermon "Soul Food," pulling a scripture passage from the Book of Psalms to prove my main point.

I felt so clever and thought that my sermon would be very relatable. After all, who *doesn't* like a good message on food for a holiday filled with memories of delectable desserts and mouth-watering dishes? But about three minutes into my message, I realized my words weren't being received as I had hoped. Instead, they went over like a lead balloon, and I was lucky I didn't put half the congregation to sleep. Afterward, my senior pastor and mentor didn't hold back.

"Kevin," he said grimly, "that was terrible."

I was crushed, and initially I couldn't figure out where I had gone wrong. I thought I had come up with something special, but I had clearly missed the mark. In retrospect, I realize I approached the whole exegetical process backward and lost sight of the importance of context.

Rather than starting with the text and applying it to people's lives, I started with my grand idea and tried to force the text to fit my interpretation. I was more interested in having people think well of me than I was in helping people understand scripture. I wanted those in the congregation to come up afterward and say, "Kevin, you did such a great job," more than I wanted them to say, "Kevin, you helped me see God's word in a way I never did before, and I am going to live differently as a result."

This experience taught me a crucial lesson. Delivering exegetically sound and contextually relevant messages wasn't just a matter of saying something I thought was interesting. It was about being true to the original scripture author's intent and applying it accurately to my audience's present-day setting.

REMEMBER THAT SMALL DECISIONS CAN BE TIPPING POINTS

Context is powerful, and it can't help but impact us. In *The Tipping Point*, Malcolm Gladwell introduces the Power of Context as a fundamental principle explaining why certain behaviors, ideas, or trends reach a tipping point. He argues that human behavior is heavily influenced by environmental factors rather than just individual personality traits.

Gladwell writes, "The Power of Context says that human beings are a lot more sensitive to their environment than they may seem."[14] Small changes in our surroundings can lead to dramatic shifts in how people act, making the context in which behavior occurs a powerful catalyst for change.

To illustrate this point, Gladwell points to the broken windows theory. This was proposed by social scientists James Q. Wilson and George L. Kelling in 1982 and suggests that visible signs of disorder and neglect in a neighborhood—like broken windows, graffiti, and litter—signal a lack of care and control, creating an environment where more serious crimes are likely to occur.

The theory argues that minor offenses and visible decay set a tone of lawlessness, encouraging further vandalism and criminal behavior. As Wilson and Kelling write,

> Muggers and robbers, whether opportunistic or professional, believe they reduce their chances of being caught or

14 Keller, *Center Church*.

> even identified if they operate on streets where potential victims are already intimidated by prevailing conditions. If the neighborhood cannot keep a bothersome panhandler from annoying passersby, the thief may reason, it is even less likely to call the police to identify a potential mugger or to interfere if the mugging actually takes place.[15]

Notice the ripple effect. If small issues are addressed, this makes for a more orderly and safe community. In essence, the Power of Context and broken windows theory emphasize that the environment shapes behavior far more than we might assume. Small, strategic changes in context can act as tipping points, setting off chain reactions that transform individual actions and, eventually, societal trends.

RECOGNIZE THAT EVERY DECISION IS INTERCONNECTED

Proper contextualization is more than just understanding the surface needs. It's about digging deep and advocating for what truly matters, even if it means making short-term sacrifices. As a leader, I believe wholeheartedly in playing the long game. In many cases, you must be willing to take a loss in some areas if it helps people feel more invested in the broader vision.

It's a bit like the challenges many cities have with gentrification. If a community leader sees a poor, "broken-window" community, their natural knee-jerk response can often be to push lower-income residents out, rebuild, and bring more affluent residents in. This leads to a rise in property values, improved amenities, and a shift in the local culture.

---

15 George L. Kelling and Catherine M. Coles, *Fixing Broken Windows* (New York: Touchstone, 1996), 20.

However, again, there is a ripple effect. "Improving" a community can result in the displacement of longtime residents who can no longer afford the increased costs, creating tension over the changes in the community's character and demographics. In fact, the broken windows theory itself is often used as justification for racial profiling and excessive force by police forces exacted upon communities of color, contributing to the mass incarceration that is leaving neighborhoods and cities in tatters. Every decision is interconnected. This was a reality I came to realize all too well.

When I stepped into the role of CEO at Frederick Douglass, I realized I would need to sacrifice some immediate losses for long-term wins. There were a lot of "broken windows" that led to a dilapidated financial situation. When our school decided to unionize the February before I became CEO, it was the first time a charter school network in Massachusetts had taken this step. It was a major development for the sector, especially for large, multisite networks.

Massachusetts is known for its challenging regulatory environment, which makes it harder for charter schools to operate independently unless they belong to a network. Other charters in the state had unionized before, usually with the UAW or IEE. However, this was the first time the Boston Teachers Union, one of the oldest teacher unions in the country, was taking on a charter school.

To say this raised alarm across the sector is an understatement. People feared that if unionization spread, it would undermine the autonomy granted by charter laws—autonomies that allowed for longer school days and the flexibility to hire teachers who weren't immediately certified. These flexibilities have been instrumental in achieving success, especially in communities of color. The concern was that unionization could erase these gains.

I was never anti-union. Both my parents are retired union members. My father was a shop steward, and I remember speaking at the board of education meeting in support of my mother's teacher union when they went on strike in August 1994. I firmly believe unions have made significant contributions to American labor, including the forty-hour work week, health benefits, and improved working conditions.

But from a sector perspective, if unionization spread to charters, it could diminish the very freedoms that allowed these schools to thrive.

RECOGNIZE THE PROS AND CONS

While I knew change wouldn't be easy, even I couldn't have anticipated the full ripple effect of the process. Frederick Douglass's unionization efforts had complex and far-reaching effects, not just on our immediate finances but on the culture and vision of the school, the dynamics with students, and the relationships we had with donors and stakeholders.

Before the union efforts began, we had consistent support from a major funder, who contributed upward of half a million dollars annually. This donor had been a reliable cornerstone of our funding structure. However, as soon as unionization became a tangible reality, he withdrew his support entirely. His stance was clear: he did not want to contribute funds that would go to teacher salaries instead of student outcomes. Other donors shared his concern and also chose not to give.

This suddenly meant we had a major gap in our budget, and for several years, we had to operate without this significant source of funding, which put a tremendous strain on our budget and operational stability. Eventually, once we reached a contract agreement, he returned as a major donor. While this was certainly a relief and gave us a sense of accomplishment in securing financial support post-unionization, that gap left a deep mark on our organization's resources during a critical period of negotiation and adjustment.

On top of this, we felt the impact of unionization on our relationship with our authorizer, the Massachusetts Board of Elementary and Secondary Education (BESE). This body is responsible for renewing charters and conducting assessments to ensure each school is meeting performance metrics and operating sustainably. Every five years, the board evaluates whether a charter school meets its stated goals and is financially viable enough to continue serving its students.

Because of the unionization negotiations and the financial strain they introduced, the BESE had legitimate concerns about whether we could remain viable. They looked closely at whether our finances would support the contract and the operational demands it introduced. The authorizer's scrutiny extended to our regular audits, which in turn affected how potential donors and philanthropists perceived us.

Many philanthropists rely on these audits to evaluate an organization's stability and viability, so when our audits raised red flags due to union-related challenges, it created hesitation in the philanthropic community. This hesitation adversely affected our fundraising efforts, further complicating our financial picture.

Our banking partners were also affected by union-related instability. At one point, our financial standing and loan terms came into question due to what's known as a technical default on one of our debt covenants. In simple terms, although we were making our loan payments on time, our financial ratios and cash flow metrics fell short of the bank's standards because the resources were being channeled toward union negotiations and operational adjustments.

While we informed the bank early on about these challenges and received verbal assurances that they understood our situation and would grant a covenant waiver, they later backtracked and placed us under a strict forbearance agreement. This agreement imposed further restrictions and required us to prove that our financial decisions aligned with maintaining the long-term health of the institution. It also meant we had to constantly reassure the bank of our stability, which consumed time and resources and further stressed our operations.

Unlike public districts, where there's a different level of state support, our charter's sustainability depended entirely on balancing our commitments to both staff and students. We were essentially building a framework that not only needed to address today's challenges but also had to hold up twenty years down the line.

PREPARE FOR THE RIPPLE EFFECT

Every word in the contract mattered because it would set a precedent for the future. I didn't want to leave a legacy where future leaders would wonder, "Why did Kevin agree to this? It doesn't make any sense." I had to think several steps ahead.

For instance, unions often operate on the principle that if they can't get the money they seek in salary increases, they'll seek more favorable contract language. This could involve things like increased sick or vacation time. The problem is that while that might seem like a good compromise in the moment, it creates long-term financial liabilities for the organization.

Let's say I can't meet a request for a 5 percent salary increase and instead offer additional vacation days. It might solve the immediate issue, but when those employees leave, the accrued vacation time may eventually become a payout obligation. This liability could be significant, potentially outweighing the savings from the smaller salary increase.

It would affect our financial health, impacting our balance sheet and potentially raising red flags during audits. This is something our authorizer and other stakeholders didn't fully appreciate. They just wanted a contract finalized quickly to move past the distraction.

However, I couldn't afford to simply agree to everything the union requested without considering the long-term impact. As with a game of chess, I had to safeguard our position several moves ahead. Each decision needed to be strategic, ensuring that we wouldn't be boxed in later by unfavorable language or precedents. It was about preserving our ability to operate effectively and autonomously, not just for a day but for years down the road.

One critical issue was the salary structure. In a unionized environment, there's typically a standardized salary scale where everyone is paid the same based on their experience, regardless of performance. However, in the charter school context, we aimed to reward strong teacher performance and differentiate and incentivize excellence. That's something traditional unions often resist. They believe all teachers should receive better compensation, which is fair, but it doesn't align with the merit-based approach many charter schools prefer.

Massachusetts is an "at-will employment" state, meaning employment can be terminated without cause, provided it's legal. In a union environment, however, there's a lengthy grievance process that adds red tape, making it harder to remove underperforming staff. Furthermore, the "last in, first out" principle means that in the event of layoffs, the most seasoned teachers' jobs are preserved even if a newer teacher has stellar student performance. These differences were significant concerns during negotiations because they clashed with the operational model that charter schools rely on.

Throughout the negotiation, I sensed the ripple effect of my decisions and felt that I was advocating not just for Frederick Douglass but for the entire charter sector in Massachusetts. Frederick Douglass Charter Public Schools, specifically, faced additional challenges. Our situation was observed across the broader educational sector, especially within the charter school networks in Boston and New Bedford.

Because there was a sense that our unionization might set a precedent that could spread to other charters, we faced intense scrutiny from our charter peers and other stakeholders. They watched us closely, analyzing every development in our negotiation process and speculating about the implications of our decisions.

Again, this meant that every term in the contract had to be meticulously evaluated for its future impact, which added yet another layer of complexity to the negotiations. Ultimately, the unionization efforts impacted nearly every aspect of our operation, from fundraising to relationships with the authorizer and the banking community, and even our internal staff dynamics.

We learned that we had to navigate these pressures while keeping our commitment to providing a stable, student-centered learning environment despite the disruptions that came with union demands. While unionization brought some hard-earned gains for our teachers and staff, the financial and operational toll it took on our institution had a ripple effect that was impossible to ignore.

COLLECT FEEDBACK AND SHOW OTHERS YOUR PROCESS

Managing these kinds of tensions requires seeing the argument from the other side. To do this, I developed a tool that's been instrumental in this process, both at church and at work. It's a simple framework I call the Recommendation Chart, and I've included it in the appendix. The chart lays out the question at hand, the deadline for action, the consequences of inaction, and the potential paths forward—typically labeled as options A, B, and C. It also includes a list of pros and cons for each option.

The challenge of using this chart is that it forces the person completing it to think through the pros and cons from multiple perspectives, not just their own. This way, when a decision is made, all the relevant context and potential outcomes are laid out on the table. Too often in organizations, decisions are made hastily, without a clear record of the rationale behind them. Then, when things go wrong, there's a lot of finger-pointing and questions about why certain choices were made.

With the Recommendation Chart, there is a documented process that explains how we arrived at a decision, based on the criteria and context considered at the time. When the baton is passed to a new leader or there is a need to review whether the decision met its desired results, there is a written record of how the decision was reached, inclusive of the factors that were considered.

RECOMMENDATION FOR ARAMCO AMERICAS PARTNERSHIP WITH THE CARVER CENTER

<table>
<tr><td>Summary of the Challenge</td><td colspan="3">• The Carver Center engaged in conversation with Aramco regarding partnership in August 2022 and explained that we were not currently accepting any new partners for the remainder of 2022.
• On January 9, Aramco sent an email indicating that they would like to become a three-year Terawatt Partner paying $450,000 up front.
• Carver Center has not yet solidified a process for how to "vet" prospective oil and gas interests.
• Aramco is one of the biggest producers of oil in the world but has begun investing in sustainability and climatetech.</td></tr>
<tr><td>Objective</td><td colspan="3">Decide whether we would like to include Aramco in our portfolio of partners based on pros and cons.</td></tr>
<tr><td>Deadline for action</td><td colspan="3">Monday, January 23, 2023 at 4 PM CT</td></tr>
<tr><td>Consequences of inaction</td><td colspan="3">Carver Center seems unorganized and unsure of its strategy. It sends a message to external partners that we do not know who we do or do not want to partner with.</td></tr>
<tr><td>Possible Paths Forward</td><td><u>Summary</u></td><td><u>Pros</u></td><td><u>Cons</u></td></tr>
<tr><td>Option A</td><td>Carver Center agrees to partner with Aramco Americas as a three-year Terawatt.</td><td>• Carver Center receives funding to continue subsidizing member startup costs.
• Carver Center startups engage more closely with Aramco and its $1.5 billion sustainability fund.
• Carver Center continues to engage key players, signaling seriousness of the decarbonization agenda in Houston.
• Carver Center fast-tracks developing its narratives around partnerships and who we partner with and why.
• Carver Center's decision could accelerate the peaceful decarbonization of a geopolitically crucial, oil-and-gas-dependent nation and larger region.</td><td>• Carver Center could be accused of "greenwashing" and receive negative press for partnering with a company owned by a problematic government.
• If New York continues to be a consideration, there might be pushback around engaging with a Saudi-based company.
• Other prospective partners might not be inclined to engage with Carver Center, whether they are in oil and gas or not.
• Carver Center's decision could confer social license to Aramco, and by extension, the Saudi government, lessening pressure to address the government's human rights abuses.
• Carver Center's decision could embolden other oil and gas partners to pursue decarbonization through innovation without addressing climate justice and other climate-related CSR issues</td></tr>
</table>

Option B	Carver Center refuses to partner with Aramco Americas.	• Carver Center does not need to worry about public perception on partnering with another oil and gas constituent and accusations of greenwashing. • Carver Center fast-tracks developing its narratives around partnerships and who we partner with and why. • Carver Center's decision could reinforce pressure on the Saudi government to correct its human rights abuses • Carver Center's decision could also send a signal to other oil and gas partners that Carver Center expects them to take a holistic view of their responsibilities as players in the energy transition, as preconditions for partnership.	• Relationship with existing Aramco employee who sits out of Carver Center Somerville, Tibor Toth, might become strained and might lead to him leaving. • Relationships with Carver Center startups that have received investment from Aramco – Syzygy, Form Energy, Amogy – might be affected. • There might be a closer microscope to who we do engage with and why and what separates them from Aramco, e.g. Shell, Chevron, bp, Vitol, etc. • Other prospective partners might not be inclined to engage with Carver Center, whether they are in oil and gas or not. • Carver Center's decision could contribute to a freezing-out of Aramco, Saudi Arabia, and the surrounding region from global decarbonization efforts, which could increase the risk that the energy transition takes a chaotic and less peaceful path in the region.
Option C	Carver Center signs a one-year agreement and bases renewal of Aramco contract on performance.	• Carver Center can monitor Aramco's interaction with itself and its startups and can act on renewing the partnership based on experience, i.e. a trial period. • Carver Center avoids the cons of Option B.	• It might be difficult and uncomfortable to explain to Aramco why Carver Center would only like to partner for one year. • Carver Center could "cancel" a three-year Terawatt contract with no legal repercussions and follow a similar path indicated in Option C while making it easier to obtain future funding if Option A is implemented.
Option D	Aramco becomes a partner at a Gigawatt or Megawatt level as opposed to Terawatt.	• Carver Center avoids a press release that circulates the announcement of the partnership. • Carver Center avoids the cons of Option B.	• Aramco gets the benefit of a Carver Center partnership without putting enough "skin in the game." • Engagement is not as deep or as meaningful as with a Terawatt level.

Recommendation	I recommend that we agree to a three-year Terawatt partnership.
Next Steps	• If Option A: o Nour to reach out to Aramco Americas to let them know of the decision. o Follow standard onboarding steps. o Use this chart to build a more robust vetting framework for prospective oil and gas and oil and gas adjacent partners. • If Option B: o Kevin or Juliana to reach out to Aramco Americas to let them know of the decision. o Return any funding that we may have received from Aramco. o Use this chart to build a more robust vetting framework for prospective oil and gas and oil and gas adjacent partners. • If Option C: o Nour to reach out to Aramco Americas to let them know of the decision. o Follow standard onboarding steps. o Use this chart to build a more robust vetting framework for prospective oil and gas and oil and gas adjacent partners. • If Option D: o Nour to reach out to Aramco Americas to let them know of the decision. o Follow standard onboarding steps. o Use this chart to build a more robust vetting framework for prospective oil and gas and oil and gas adjacent partners.

A related tool I've found valuable is Bain Capital's RAPID decision-making framework—which stands for Recommender, Approver, Performer, Input Provider, and Decision Maker. What I appreciate about RAPID is that it explicitly values input without confusing it for decision-making rights. Input provides context, information, and a voice at the table, but it doesn't mean the person giving input makes the final call. This distinction is critical in any decision-making process.

The RAPID framework identifies the roles each stakeholder plays in a decision

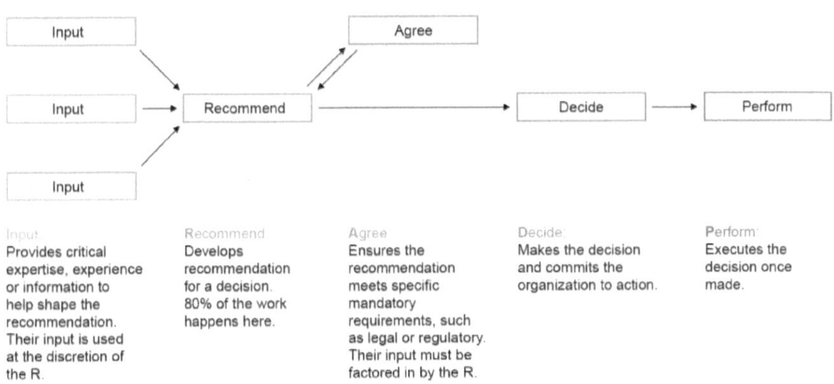

RAPID® is a registered trademark of Bain & Company

The Recommendation Chart incorporates this principle. By listing the pros and cons of each option and clearly stating whose input was considered, we ensure that even if people don't agree with the final decision, they know their perspectives were included. It's a way of saying "We heard you."

It's like when you ask your kids what they want for dinner—one says pizza, another says tacos, and a third says spaghetti. In the end, you might decide on burgers. It doesn't mean you ignored their preferences. It just means you weighed all the options and made the best decision for everyone.

In both work and personal life, I've found that people are more willing to accept a decision if they trust the process and see how the decisions your team is making today fit into the context of the grander company mission statement and vision. They might not like every outcome, but they can respect it if they believe their input was genuinely considered. That's the essence of managing tensions—balancing the needs and wants of all parties while staying true to your core priorities. It's not about pleasing everyone; it's about building trust through a fair and transparent process.

The Recommendation Chart has served me pastorally as well, as when People's Institutional AME Church in Brooklyn decided whether to sell the parsonage and use the proceeds to complete needed repairs to the worship facility and adjacent properties. Or when Israel AME Church in Albany was faced with the question of whether to rent its parsonage and use the monthly rent to mitigate against fluctuations in member giving as well as to pay down its debt. Also, to be clear, there was not unanimity in any of these votes, but the members, officers, and leaders of our church could trust the process and that the context had been fully considered in the final outcome.

REMEMBER: THE BEST DECISIONS ARE ALWAYS MADE IN PROPER CONTEXT

Leadership is messy, but if you're able to keep track of the broader picture, your job will be made much easier. Context isn't just helpful—it's essential.

So, before taking any bold steps, study your material thoroughly to ensure you have a full grasp of the situation. Whether you're leading a meeting, negotiating a contract, or delivering a message, deep knowledge equips you to anticipate challenges and make more thoughtful, informed choices. Without a thorough understanding, it's easy to miss key details that could drastically impact the outcome.

Next, focus on what's most important. Context adds depth, but the core message must be clear and straightforward. It's easy to get lost in the details, but effective leaders know how to extract the most important insights and present them concisely. When you zero in on what truly matters, you communicate with precision, cutting through the noise and guiding others toward the best course of action.

Finally, use context to connect and communicate effectively. Exegete your church or business organization. Understand the setting, key players, and key dynamics at work. By grounding your decisions and explanations in context, you build trust and credibility, showing that you've considered the full picture.

It's this nuanced understanding that allows you to communicate in a way that resonates, aligns others with your vision, and leads to sound, sustainable decisions.

BULLETIN NOTES

KEY TAKEAWAYS:

- ☑ Context is crucial for sound decision-making, as it ensures accurate understanding and prevents misinterpretation.
- ☑ Exegesis seeks the original meaning based on context, while eisegesis imposes personal biases, leading to subjective interpretations.
- ☑ Small changes in context can trigger significant behavioral shifts, highlighting the importance of understanding interconnected systems.
- ☑ Transparent decision-making processes, using tools like the Recommendation Chart, build trust by considering diverse perspectives and documenting the rationale.

KEY QUESTIONS:

1. How can leaders ensure they are consistently applying exegesis rather than eisegesis in their interpretation of data?
2. What specific strategies can be implemented to anticipate and manage the ripple effects of decisions in a complex organizational environment?
3. How can leaders effectively balance short-term sacrifices for long-term gains while maintaining the trust and support of stakeholders?

PRINCIPLE 3

Stability Is the Backbone of Every Successful Organization

True stability results when presumed order and presumed disorder are balanced. A truly stable system expects the unexpected, is prepared to be disrupted, waits to be transformed.

—TOM ROBBINS

Instability is *the* major problem with almost every unsuccessful organization. Show me a church or company that has shaky leadership, shaky finances, or shaky decision-making, and I will show you an organization that is on the ropes.

Stability provides a foundation upon which an organization can grow, innovate, and adapt to changing circumstances. Without stability, even the most promising organizations can falter due to internal chaos, low morale, and ineffective operations. As Ralph Waldo Emerson said, "All great natures delight in stability."[16]

When employees feel secure in their roles and understand the organization's direction, they are more likely to be engaged and

16 Ralph Waldo Emerson, *The Later Lectures of Ralph Waldo Emerson, 1843–1871* (Athens, GA: University of Georgia Press, 2010), 34.

motivated. This engagement leads to higher productivity, better teamwork, and a stronger commitment to the organization's goals. Stability also enhances an organization's reputation with external stakeholders, including customers, investors, and partners.

A stable organization is perceived as reliable and trustworthy, making others more willing to invest time and resources into collaborative efforts. Furthermore, a stable organization is better equipped to handle crises and unexpected challenges. With clear protocols and a solid leadership structure in place, the organization can respond effectively without descending into confusion.

Organizations that prioritize stability are more likely to achieve sustained success and make a lasting impact in their industries.

STABILITY STARTS WITH A COMPELLING VISION

As a pastor, I've stepped into several unstable church environments. When I do, one of the first steps I take is to read *Rich Church, Poor Church* with my officers and ministerial staff. It's a fantastic short book that gets straight to the point about what it means to be a "rich" church. And by rich, I don't mean financially wealthy. I'm talking about having a growth mindset, a focus on meeting the community's needs, and a willingness to engage in meaningful ministry.

In these pages, J. Clif Christopher explores the contrasting financial health of congregations and identifies key factors that distinguish thriving churches from those struggling with finances. His primary argument is that churches with strong, consistent giving are those that effectively communicate a compelling vision, build genuine relationships with their members, and prioritize transparency in financial matters.

Christopher contrasts this with "poor" churches, which often lack clear vision, shy away from discussing finances, and fail to engage with members personally, leading to stagnation. Several pages into this book, Christopher shares this powerful story that has stuck with me for years. As someone who was often asked to consult with local churches, he writes,

> I was at an initial assessment of a church, sitting in the pastor's office. As we reviewed data that he had previously sent, I noted the church's mission statement: "We will make disciples of Jesus Christ for the transformation of the world."
>
> I said to him, "That is a very biblical mission statement."
>
> He seemed pleased at my compliment and went on to say that it was not very original but it had been adopted by the church at a leadership retreat the previous year. We continued to review what was going on in this church. The demographics showed that it was in a growing area that had numerous young families living within a couple of miles of the church. A junior high school was located one block down and across the street. Visibility was good, and their facility was more than adequate to accommodate growth.
>
> I then asked him, "As the pastor, who do you feel is without Christ in your community that you need to minister to the most?"
>
> He quickly shot back, "Oh, we all know it is the young families. They are really struggling with raising their kids, paying the bills, keeping marriages together, and all those young-family issues."
>
> I then commented to him that the average age of his church was close to sixty and that it did not seem that many

> of those young families were a part of the church now nor were they about to join anytime soon. He agreed.
>
> "Therefore," I said, "How do you see the church fulfilling its mission?"
>
> "I want to start a more contemporary service, weekday child care, and an Upward basketball program."
>
> "Well," I said, "that sounds like some excellent ideas to excite and get you in front of that crowd. What is stopping you?"
>
> "The Simpsons and the Walkers," he said. "They are vehemently opposed to any sort of worship that is not traditional and does not use the hymnbook. The child care program might get through, but no basketball, because Rotary and one other group use our hall and it would require too much maintenance money to keep it clean."
>
> I looked a bit stunned, and he shook his head.
>
> "But what about the mission of making disciples?" I asked.
>
> "That is the mission on paper because it looks good. The real mission of this church is to make sure that these two families are kept happy and that their money keeps flowing. They make a big deal of paying all of our denominational dues each year. No one else wants to risk losing that money. There are certainly some folks who don't like this, but no one wants to be the one who takes responsibility or the nails on this one."[17]

What had happened? This church had missed the bigger picture. They'd allowed two families to destabilize their entire model of outreach and distract them from their primary mission.

---

17 J. Clif Christopher, *Rich Church, Poor Church: Keys to Effective Financial Ministry* (Nashville: Abingdon Press, 2012), 20–22.

Reading *Rich Church, Poor Church* with my officers and ministerial staff helps reveal where they stand in their understanding of ministry. It helps shift their mindset from a scarcity mentality to one of abundance and opportunity. It also challenges the outdated view that denominational assessments and legacy preservation are the main reasons people give to the church. Those days are over.

People now have choices about where to donate their money, and they expect to see a tangible impact from their contributions. Many view a donation to the church the same as a donation to an organization like the United Way or Red Cross. They want to see how their giving makes a difference. So, during the offering, instead of trying to bring church stability by obsessively talking about bills and financial needs, I bring stability by casting a compelling vision and talking about the impact our church is making on the community.

For instance, my current church, Israel AME in Albany, provides book scholarships and care packages to college students every year. I ask the students to send thank-you notes, and then I read those notes during the offering. I'll say, "We've received another thank-you note from one of our students who was touched by your generosity. They felt supported and loved by their church family."

This way, I'm reminding the congregation that their giving is making a difference, that it's more than just paying bills—it's about changing lives. As a result, congregants and visitors alike are more motivated to give when they see the impact.

Unfortunately, when any organization is unstable, the knee-jerk response of many leaders is to double down on what is driving the instability. Case in point, when I reviewed the financials after being assigned to one of my previous churches, I found it odd that they had a special offering *every* fourth Sunday.

When I asked about this, the leaders told me that this was the day the former pastor would stand before the congregation and essentially beg for financial donations to keep the lights (or heat or water) on. She told everyone that if they didn't raise enough money, the lights would be turned off. Her go-to solution was to ask ten or twelve people to give $100 each, and month after month, they managed to scrape it together to keep the utilities from shutting off.

One need only imagine how destabilizing this approach was for new visitors or potential converts to Christianity. If the first thing a new person heard when they walked into a church was that the congregation couldn't pay the light bill, this wouldn't exactly inspire confidence. From years of experience, I knew that many people came to church looking for help with their own struggles, whether it was paying their own bills or dealing with family issues. If the church couldn't even manage its own finances, how could it help anyone else? These actions sent the message that the church wasn't well maintained or capable of addressing real problems.

Instead, when you focus on creating a compelling vision and establishing a standard of excellence, this drives generosity and stability. When you set the bar high, people will either rise to meet it or step aside. I've seen it time and again: officers who aren't engaged in the work often decide it's too much for them. They'll say, "I'm not sure I'm on the right track here; I think I need to step down." And that's OK, because it leaves room for those who are committed to rise and take action.

In every church I've served, this has proven true. When we prioritize real, impactful ministry, we create a culture of growth and engagement. People are drawn to that, and financial stability follows naturally. It's all about changing the mindset from scarcity to abundance, from merely surviving to thriving, from chasing dollars to being captivated by a compelling vision.

WITHOUT STABILITY, ORGANIZATIONS FALL APART

When stability isn't prioritized, the results can be disastrous. A few years ago, I had an experience that really drove this point home. As we have discussed in chapter 1, during my time at Frederick Douglass, I saw how a lack of stability—often caused by well-meaning but misinformed philanthropic efforts—could derail progress. Curious about whether these same issues existed in other fields, I moved into the clean energy sector and joined the Carver Center for Climate Justice.

I was drawn to the Carver Center because I wanted to see how philanthropy was influencing the rapidly growing climate tech space and if there were applicable lessons learned from the role of philanthropy in the charter school space. The Carver Center is a nonprofit incubator supporting start-ups that are developing new technologies to fight climate change. They provide resources and community support to help entrepreneurs build and scale their businesses.

These incubators provide start-ups with prototyping labs, office spaces, and community resources essential for developing and scaling solutions to combat climate change. Since its inception, the Carver Center has supported over five hundred start-ups, boasting a 90 percent survival rate among them, and has facilitated the creation of more than eleven thousand jobs. The organization emphasizes inclusivity and collaboration, offering programs such as partnership accelerators and initiatives supporting BIPOC-led start-ups, all aimed at driving impactful climate action.

When I got to the Carver Center, it was clear there were some big disparities. Most of the entrepreneurs were from elite schools like nearby Harvard and MIT, and they had family money to back them up. Meanwhile, students from historically Black colleges and universities, like the one I attended, often didn't have the same financial safety net. This was a problem, because communities of color are the ones most affected by climate change, yet they were barely represented in the room when it came to developing solutions. It felt similar to what I'd seen in charter schools—well-intentioned efforts missing the mark because the people most affected weren't at the table.

I started at the Carver Center as the CFO and then stepped in as interim CEO when the previous leader stepped down from her role. I quickly realized there was a major issue with stability, especially in the executive team. The organization had been built around its founder, and when she left unexpectedly, there wasn't a solid plan for what would come next. The COO, who was well liked but part of some systemic issues, had been let go a few months earlier, and that created a lot of unrest. Staff members felt ignored and wrote to the board, saying they weren't being heard. This lack of stability became a serious problem as we tried to move forward.

One of the biggest challenges was what's known as the "founder's dilemma." The founder's departure left a big gap, and we struggled to figure out how to keep things moving without her driving the mission. To help bring some stability, I started initiatives like the Between the Lines book club, where we read Jim Collins's *Good to Great.* This book focuses on what makes some companies achieve long-term success while others don't. One of its key lessons is about getting the right people on the bus and creating a culture of discipline. As Collins writes,

> The executives who ignited the transformations from good to great did not first figure out where to drive the bus and then get people to take it there. No, they first got the right people on the bus (and the wrong people off the bus) and then figured out where to drive it. They said, in essence, "Look, I don't really know where we should take this bus. But

> I know this much: If we get the right people on the bus, the right people in the right seats, and the wrong people off the bus, then we'll figure out how to take it someplace great."[18]

As it turned out, getting people in the right seat was especially difficult. The COVID-19 pandemic only worsened the problem. During this time, the Carver Center made a bold decision to expand from Somerville, Massachusetts, to Houston, Texas—right into the heart of the oil and gas industry. While it was the right strategic move, it brought new challenges and instability.

By the time I joined the Carver Center in 2022, we were operating in a region that historically didn't align with our mission to fight climate change. There were also small but impactful issues, like time zone differences, that made our Texas team feel left out of the loop. This created tension between the two offices, and it became clear that without a stable, inclusive approach, we were at risk of losing our focus.

Things came to a head when I decided to engage with oil and gas companies, including a partnership with Aramco Americas, a subsidiary of Saudi Aramco, one of the largest oil companies in the world. It was a controversial move and made headlines in the *Boston Globe*. The partnership deal was worth $450,000—not huge, but Saudi Aramco set aside billions for clean energy initiatives.

As noted in the Recommendation Chart found in the appendix, despite the human rights violations of the nation of Saudi Arabia, I decided we needed to engage with them if we were serious about operating in Houston and making a real impact. Unfortunately, some Carver Center board members were furious, calling it a deal with the devil. But the reality is that executives from these companies who were responsible for the environmental challenge now have children

---

18 Jim Collins, *Good to Great: Why Some Companies Make the Leap ... And Others Don't* (New York: HarperCollins, 2011), 41.

working for those same organizations who are pushing them to make changes. Ignoring them wasn't a realistic strategy.

Ultimately, my decision to partner with Aramco indirectly or directly led to my departure. They brought in a new CEO, but within nine months, he quit, facing the same issues I had flagged. The organization ended up laying off a large part of the staff, and it's still struggling today. My experience was frustrating because it felt like my concerns were brushed aside.

After leaving the Carver Center, I became the interim executive director of a well-known child development center in Hartford. There, I saw another opportunity to create stability, this time through programs for kids of color. I learned about initiatives like Hartford Promise, which offers $20,000 scholarships, and Connecticut's Baby Bond program, which sets aside $20,000 for kids born into low-income families. Combined, that's $40,000—enough to start a small business or fund education or purchase a home in the state. It's a powerful way to give these kids a stable foundation for their futures.

I wrote an op-ed connecting my decision to partner with Aramco Americas to the work I was doing at the Sarah Allen Early Childhood Center, arguing that we shouldn't shy away from support if it could help build stability for our programs.[19] Surely an organization founded by minister's wives in 1907 could understand the need for redemption, grace, and second chances.

The board didn't see it that way, accusing me of being too political. Even after I secured a $715,000 federal grant recommendation for an outdoor STEAM Lab—the largest gift in the organization's history—they dismissed my ideas as impractical. Even after I showed them

19 Rev. Kevin T. Taylor, "Opinion: Why We Should Accept 'Oil Money' to Support Climate Action and a Better Future," *Hartford Courant*, May 23, 2024, https://www.courant.com/author/rev-kevin-t-taylor/.

how their investment portfolio grew in large part to the organization's holdings in stocks and bonds in the oil industry, they were unmoved.

Through all these experiences, I've learned that stability is the backbone of any organization that wants to succeed. Without a stable leadership structure, clear plans for succession, and a commitment to inclusivity, even the best intentions can lead to chaos. My time at the Carver Center and beyond has reinforced the lesson that a solid, stable foundation is what allows organizations to thrive, innovate, and make a lasting impact. Stability isn't about resisting change. It's about creating a strong platform that can adapt and grow, no matter what challenges arise.

HAVE THE CRUCIAL CONVERSATIONS

The challenge of trying to bring stability to an organization is that your voice can be unsettling since it bucks the status quo. As someone who has what I'd describe as "prophetic" tendencies, I naturally speak truth to power. It's this mindset that cost me two jobs because of my unpopular stance on working with Aramco Americas.

I've faced a lot of backlash for being outspoken. People have labeled me as too radical, even unemployable. This can be tough to hear. Still, I feel a responsibility as a Christian and a leader to speak out against injustice. It's part of my calling, even if it comes with risks.

In the Message translation, Jeremiah 1:9–10 says, "God reached out, touched my mouth, and said, 'Look! I've just put my words in your mouth—hand-delivered! See what I've done? I've given you a job to do among nations and governments—a red-letter day! Your job is to pull up and tear down, take apart and demolish. And then start over, building and planting.'"

While these words were spoken to the prophet Jeremiah, they are applicable to my life as well. Jeremiah used his prophetic voice to encourage people to return to God's ways and speak truth to power. Likewise, my prophetic voice has opened doors I wouldn't have otherwise, but it has also cost me deeply. I'm committed to communicating challenges and speaking up when I feel things need to change.

During my time at the Carver Center, I created space for our team to read *Crucial Conversations*. The reason I chose it was that we had a deeper problem: a complete lack of clear feedback and communication. As the authors write, "At the core of every successful conversation lies the free flow of relevant information. People openly and honestly express their opinions, share their feelings, and articulate their theories. They willingly and capably share their views, even when their ideas are controversial or unpopular."[20]

In smaller organizations like the Carver Center, promotions often happen without any clear criteria, leading to confusion and frustration. People felt that favorites were being promoted without transparency about what was needed to advance. There was no clear path for moving from manager to senior manager or from senior manager to director. This lack of clarity bred resentment and distrust among the staff.

I wanted to change that by piloting a program to provide training for senior managers and directors. The goal was to establish a baseline of skills and competencies required at each level, giving people a clearer, more structured path for career growth. In my view, while the executive team was dysfunctional, the real leadership potential was with the managers and directors. By equipping them with the right skills, they'd be ready to step up when the time came.

---

20 Kerry Patterson, Joseph Grenny, Ron McMillan, and Al Switzler, *Crucial Conversations: Tools for Talking When Stakes Are High*, 2nd ed. (New York: McGraw-Hill, 2011), 23.

A major issue with the executive team—and the organization more broadly—was their inability to adhere to one of the key tenets of executive leadership: to give and receive honest feedback. Instead of addressing conflicts directly, they'd brush them aside, saying they were "over it." But they weren't. Old grievances would resurface in meetings, creating unnecessary tension. Executives started feeling like they had to be involved in every discussion, not because they needed to be but to defend their team members from potential criticism. It was a cycle of distrust fueled by the absence of open communication.

I saw similar problems at the child development center. Although it was an organization with over a century of history and service to the community, the staff had deep-seated conflicts. They had worked together for years but were constantly at odds, mainly because they had never learned how to give or receive feedback properly. People kept doing things that annoyed their colleagues simply because no one had ever told them it was a problem. It was a classic case of unspoken frustrations simmering below the surface.

Despite these challenges, I'm more convinced than ever that the key to long-term stability is through short-term pain. Stability isn't about ensuring everyone is happy. It's about knowing where the organization needs to go, creating collective buy-in, and having those crucial conversations to help everyone row in the same direction.

REMEMBER: STABILITY IS THE BACKBONE OF EVERY SUCCESSFUL ORGANIZATION

Stability in any organization begins with people. It grows when individuals feel seen, valued, and connected to a greater purpose. Helping people see themselves in the mission, whether through scripture, an organization's vision, or a shared story, strengthens their commitment. When they understand their role and how their efforts contribute to a larger goal, they are more likely to stay engaged and motivated. As Simon Sinek writes,

> Compared to a culture in which the leaders incentivize reactionary decisions or activities that focus on immediate gratification, a culture in which the selfless chemicals can flow more freely results in greater organizational stability and better long-term performance. And when that happens, our bonds grow stronger, our loyalties grow deeper and the organization gains longevity. Best of all, we go home happier and live longer and healthier as a result.[21]

True transformation takes time. Significant change rarely happens all at once. Progress often unfolds in small, steady steps, and those steps deserve recognition. Moving from a C to a B is still progress, just like increasing your charitable giving from 5 percent to 6 percent of gross income is progress. Acknowledging these wins creates momentum and builds trust, allowing for continued growth without alienating those who are part of the process. Sustainable change requires patience and a willingness to invest in the long game.

Leadership also demands a steadfast commitment to love and respect, even in challenging situations. As Mark Sanborn writes, "The most important thing is love of others. Not necessarily a sugary, let's-all-sing-'We-Are-the-World' kind of love, but a stable, meaningful generosity of spirit that enables us to

21 Simon Sinek, *Leaders Eat Last: Why Some Teams Pull Together and Others Don't* (New York: Penguin Publishing Group, 2014), 75.

> do things for others—those we know and those we don't—because at base level we choose to give of ourselves."[22]

People may resist change or even work against you, but consistent acts of kindness and care can open doors to trust and understanding. Simple gestures, such as sending cards to every member of a congregation as I do at church, or to each team member as I do at work, reinforce the message that they matter, regardless of their stance or level of support. This consistency in care helps create a sense of stability and strengthens relationships over time.

By grounding leadership in these principles—helping people see their roles in the mission, embracing gradual progress, and leading with unwavering care—organizations can establish a foundation that endures. Stability isn't about avoiding challenges or maintaining the status quo. It's about cultivating a shared sense of purpose and creating an environment where growth and connection thrive. Through thoughtful leadership and intentional actions, your church, nonprofit, or business can navigate challenges and inspire lasting impact for the future.

BULLETIN NOTES

KEY TAKEAWAYS:

- ☑ Stability is crucial for enabling organizations to innovate, grow, and navigate challenges without falling into chaos or uncertainty.
- ☑ A clear and compelling vision aligns efforts toward a shared purpose and helps people feel personally connected to the organization's mission.

---

22 Mark Sanborn, *The Fred Factor: How Passion in Your Work and Life Can Turn the Ordinary into the Extraordinary* (New York: Crown, 2004), 114.

- ☑ Sustainable success comes through incremental progress, where celebrating small wins builds trust and momentum for lasting change.
- ☑ Leadership based on kindness, respect, and consistency strengthens relationships and fosters a resilient, united community.

KEY QUESTIONS:

1. How can leaders help individuals in their organization see themselves as part of the mission or vision, fostering a deeper sense of commitment and belonging?
2. What specific strategies can organizations adopt to address resistance to change while maintaining stability and trust among stakeholders?
3. How can leaders balance the need for immediate action with a long-term focus on gradual progress to ensure sustainable transformation?

PRINCIPLE 4

Get to Know Your People

The best way to find yourself is to lose yourself in the service of others.

—MAHATMA GANDHI

The best way to know how you should lead others is by getting to know the others you lead.

Any leader can step into an organization with a vision for how they want to bring change, but it takes a great leader to get to know the hearts of their people. As Dale Carnegie wrote, "You can make more friends in two months by becoming interested in other people than you can in two years by trying to get other people interested in you."[23]

When we take the time to understand other people's experiences, values, and perspectives, we open ourselves up to diverse viewpoints and ideas. In personal relationships, knowing others allows for stronger bonds and a greater sense of belonging. Whether it's with family, friends, or romantic partners, understanding each other's strengths, weaknesses, and motivations helps us navigate conflicts, celebrate successes, and provide emotional support during challenging times.

23 Dale Carnegie, *The Leader in You* (New York: Simon & Schuster, 2012), 41.

In professional settings, getting to know colleagues and clients can lead to more effective teamwork, better communication, increased productivity, and greater profitability.[24] When individuals feel understood and valued, they are more likely to contribute positively, share innovative ideas, and remain committed to shared goals. Building strong professional relationships also facilitates networking opportunities, career advancement, and a more harmonious workplace culture.

Moreover, in a broader societal context, taking the time to get to know people from different backgrounds and cultures promotes tolerance and reduces prejudice. It helps break down stereotypes, reduces microaggressions, and leads to a more cohesive and cooperative community.

HONOR THOSE YOU LEAD

When I was first appointed to a new pastoral charge, one of the most pressing challenges I faced was truly knowing my congregation. I realized that understanding who the members were, their relationships, and their individual stories was essential for building a strong, connected community. So, one of my first actions was to send postcards to everyone on the church's mailing list, and I have continued this tradition to this day by sending a postcard to every new church member.

On each card, I included questions asking for names, mailing addresses, phone numbers, emails, the number of children and grandchildren they had, the date of their wedding anniversary, whether they were veterans, any church offices they'd held, the ministries they'd

24 Lynda Gratton and Tamara J. Erickson, "Eight Ways to Build Collaborative Teams," *Harvard Business Review*, November 2007, https://hbr.org/2007/11/eight-ways-to-build-collaborative-teams.

been involved in, and what they hoped to see happen in the church. This effort not only allowed our church to verify contact information but also gave me insights into who my congregation members were beyond their attendance on Sundays.

The data collected through postcards allows us to create initiatives that recognize and celebrate our members in meaningful ways. For example, every year we host a celebration on Grandparents' Day called Three-Score and Ten to honor members who are seventy and older. This is inspired by Psalm 90:10, which says in the King James Version, "The days of our years are threescore years and ten."

Whether through small tokens like corsages or more elaborate gestures like crowns and tiaras—or gold and silver medals during Olympic years—these efforts let our seniors know they are cherished. These celebrations often bring joy not only to those being honored but also to their families and the wider congregation, reinforcing the bonds of community.

Similarly, as a CEO I used the information my team had on file to send handwritten birthday cards and personalized notes on work anniversaries. These small gestures expressed gratitude and showed that I valued individuals not just for their work but for who they were.

There are so many ways to do this in pastoring and organizational leadership. In the church, knowing who our veterans are ensures that we can appropriately honor their service. Their contributions to our nation and our congregation allow us to show our appreciation in a meaningful way.

In the workplace, I've implemented similar practices by sending thank-you cards during Thanksgiving, inspired by methods I observed at Denmark Vesey Charter Public Schools. Rather than relying on generic emails, I take the time to highlight each team member's unique contributions to the organization. These personalized notes go a long way toward making employees feel valued and appreciated, strengthening their connection to the team.

Holidays and special occasions also offer opportunities to reinforce these connections. In the church, I send seasonal greetings for events like Christmas, Easter, and Thanksgiving, ensuring that every member feels remembered during these meaningful times. For our older members or those who are homebound, these gestures often serve as a lifeline, reminding them that they are still part of the community even if they cannot attend services in person.

Similarly, in addition to sending Mother's Day and Father's Day cards, I also send sympathy cards to those who have lost their sons or daughters, mothers or fathers in the past year. Likewise, at Christmastime, I present each family that was bereaved in that calendar year with a memorial poem, given that the holiday season is especially difficult for grieving loved ones. This practice expanded during the pandemic so that we now have a memorial video with pictures of the people in our church family and extended family who have passed. In 2024, for example, the video featured nearly three hundred people, which was three-fifths of the sympathy cards I sent that year.

In the organizations I've led, I've carried out similar traditions by sending New Year's cards with messages of encouragement and optimism. These cards help set the tone for the year ahead, reminding team members that their contributions matter and that their well-being is a priority. The key is to be consistent.

The impact of these gestures has been profound. Families in the church often share how much it means to receive their monthly get-well cards for loved ones who are sick or homebound. These simple acts of kindness remind them that they are not alone during difficult times. Similarly, employees have expressed gratitude for the personal attention they've received, noting how these small yet significant actions make them feel cared for as individuals, not just as workers.

By taking the time to connect with people on a personal level, I've been able to create environments—both in the church and in the workplace—where individuals feel seen, valued, and supported. As Kirsten Weir writes on the American Psychological Association's website, "People want to know that they matter, and that they're spending their time doing work that makes a difference."[25]

EVALUATE AND ESTABLISH TRUST

When you take on a new role, I recommend giving each team member at least six months in their present role (a full year in their position at church) before making any personnel changes. This approach allows them to decide if they want to continue serving or if it's time for new members to step in. It also ensures that those who serve are doing so out of genuine desire rather than obligation.

During this time, evaluate the true intentions and commitments of those around you. As I've discovered, not everyone who smiles and says they support me may have my best interests at heart. Similarly, those who appear quiet or reserved may have a deep willingness to serve but need the right environment to step forward.

One of the tricky dynamics many pastors face is that they step into settings where they are outsiders walking into a tight-knit community. Church relational dynamics are unique and often run deeper than the pastor's role. I like to say that in most church communities, blood is thicker than communion wine. What I mean is that

---

25 Kirsten Weir, "Making a Difference at Work," American Psychological Association, accessed December 18, 2024, https://www.apa.org/topics/healthy-workplaces/making-difference-at-work.

even though Christians should believe that spiritual ties are stronger than physical ties, the reality is that family dynamics are greater than most pastors realize.

Just because I'm now some church's new pastor doesn't mean I've earned the trust of those in the congregation. Just as I am evaluating those I lead, they are evaluating me. In *The SPEED of Trust*, Stephen Covey wrote, "The first job of a leader is to inspire trust. The ability to do so, in fact, is a prime differentiator between a manager and a leader. To inspire trust is to create the foundation upon which all truly successful enterprises—and relationships—stand."[26]

Getting to know your people is more than just collecting data. It's about building meaningful relationships, recognizing and celebrating individual lives, and fostering a supportive and connected community. By taking the time to understand each member's unique story and needs, you create a church environment where everyone feels valued and engaged.

RECOGNIZE WHO IS IN AND WHO IS OUT

Trust is formed only through establishing regular, meaningful interactions. When I was a CEO, this meant initiating monthly meetings across all departments, observing direct reports in their meetings with their direct reports, and creating space for emerging leaders to interact with me. In our denomination, the pastor is the ex-officio leader of every organization but typically leads the Steward Board and the Trustee Board ministries in partnership with the vice chairs of the organizations.

---

26 Stephen M. R. Covey and Rebecca R. Merrill, *The SPEED of Trust: The One Thing That Changes Everything* (New York: Free Press, 2006), 300.

During these monthly meetings, it becomes clear who is contributing, where the information comes from, and how decisions are being made within the church. Furthermore, in our monthly official board meetings—a gathering of all organization presidents and congregants—we discuss participation, financial reporting, recurring questions, and upcoming events and provide constructive feedback on the events in the life of the church since our last meeting. This process helps us understand each person's perspective and frame of reference.

Additionally, reading resources like *Rich Church, Poor Church* exposes our leadership team to the concept of a rich church mentality, encouraging them to reflect on their priorities. Another valuable resource is the book *Why Church Matters*, by Joshua Harris.[27] Resources like these encourage our members to think deeply about giving, service, and active discipleship beyond merely attending church.

I also emphasize the importance of community service projects as part of our annual activities. For example, at the church I pastored in Brooklyn, each organization had an annual day—that is, a date on the calendar each year to celebrate their organization's anniversary and for its members to serve as liturgists during morning worship. The floral ministry, for instance, focused solely on maintaining the church's exterior, which wasn't always successful. I proposed that instead of just beautifying our own space, we should extend our efforts to the entire neighborhood. We began distributing potted plants to every home on our block with notes that included scriptures and invitations to join our church. This not only improved the neighborhood's appearance but also strengthened our community ties and brought joy to those who received the plants.

27 In *Why Church Matters*, Joshua Harris emphasizes the importance of committing to a local church community as a vital expression of faith, fostering spiritual growth, accountability, and meaningful relationships within the body of Christ.

Another initiative involved leveraging our members' strong ties to their Southern roots. Even though many of our members had moved from states like North Carolina and South Carolina to New York, they still had a deep connection to their home states. So, we decided to use some of the offerings from our South Carolina Club Annual Day to support the eight historically Black colleges and universities in that state through book scholarships. This not only honored our members' heritage but also made a tangible difference in the lives of students in those states.

Additionally, we invited South Carolina students from local universities to our church events, providing them with a sense of home and community away from their families. These efforts fostered a supportive environment and demonstrated our commitment to making a positive impact. And as the thank-you notes began coming in from scholarship recipients or college students finding a home away from home, I read them during the morning offering as a reminder that the congregation's giving was making a difference.

Through these initiatives, it became clear who was involved and who was not.

BE AN ORIGINAL

Every leader's means of getting to know their people is different. Some do this naturally; others struggle. Some leaders are charismatic and charming; others are more behind the scenes. Regardless of which category you fall into, take this advice from one of my mentors, Bishop Julius Harrison McAllister Sr.

More than once, he's looked at me and said, "Reverend Taylor, we're busy trying to be duplicates when God has called us to be originals." This statement reinforces a message I've been telling myself over the years that I don't have to mimic someone else's leadership style. I can just be me.

Contrary to the adage that imitation is the best form of flattery, there is no one else like me, and my unique gifts are what God wants me to bring to the table. Instead of trying to mimic what others are doing, I should focus on who God has called us to be and the unique contributions I can make. This perspective has been invaluable in guiding my approach to ministry.

One of the challenges for many American pastors these days is that they feel a sense of imposter syndrome. This is in part due to the rise of social media and the "cool church" culture that has emerged over the past few decades. Now, every pastor can go online and compare themselves to others. This leads them to feel discouraged when they don't measure up to the successes of others. They don't have as many numbers, as many frills, and as much money. But it's here that they need to remember those words from Bishop McAllister and focus on being originals.

While I don't lead a massive congregation, I've found great fulfillment in serving those God has entrusted me to lead. I may not be able to compete with churches that provide a concert-like atmosphere. But I can know people's names, build meaningful relationships, and shepherd them as God leads me. You can do the same.

UNDERSTAND THEIR MOTIVATIONS

For you as a leader, a large part of getting to know your people is understanding their motivations. What makes them tick? What are they passionate about? What are their greatest priorities outside the office? This is true in church, in business, and in life. At its core, leadership in any environment involves uncovering what drives people and fostering a sense of purpose and belonging.

At the Carver Center, we implemented a system to recognize culture champions and those employees who embodied our organizational values. Each month, team members voted for individuals who best represented our core principles. Winners received a traveling trophy to display on their desks, followed by a personal thank-you note from me congratulating them on their achievements.

This system didn't just celebrate accomplishments; it reinforced our values, encouraged camaraderie, and built mutual respect among colleagues. By making recognition peer driven, it removed perceptions of favoritism and ensured that acknowledgment was rooted in genuine contributions to our culture. This approach supported the deeper goal of understanding and celebrating what motivates individuals: the desire to feel valued, respected, and aligned with a meaningful purpose.

Going beyond formal recognition, I prioritized learning about what inspired and drove each team member on a personal level. Whether it was discovering that someone was training for a marathon, pursuing a professional certification, or navigating personal challenges, I made it a point to connect with their individual stories.

For instance, when a colleague in a previous organization struggled to find childcare on the day of a mission-critical meeting, I stepped in to babysit her child so she could fully engage. This act wasn't about grand gestures but about showing that their needs and aspirations were seen, valued, and supported.

When those you lead feel their struggles are empathized with, their successes are celebrated, and they are part of a cohesive team, their intrinsic motivation to contribute is amplified. As a leader, I try to build a team where everyone's unique motivations and needs are recognized, helping create a shared sense of purpose and responsibility. When I take the time to understand what drives each person, it's easier to help them grow and thrive—not just in their careers but in life. Whether it's sending a handwritten "You Rock" card, supporting their goals, or being there during tough times, I want to create an environment where people feel confident and motivated to succeed.

This kind of approach doesn't just make individuals happier; it makes the whole team stronger. When people feel understood and supported, they bring their best energy and ideas to the table so everyone can benefit. It's like being part of a community where everyone's strengths and efforts come together to create something great.

ONE BITE AT A TIME

Again, some leaders do this well, while others struggle. If you're a leader who struggles to get to know those you lead, I'd encourage you to take incremental steps. How do you run a marathon? One step at a time.

It's important not to compare yourself to others who may go above and beyond in recognition. Just because I send cards to every staff member doesn't mean you're a bad leader if you don't do the same. Instead, it's about finding authentic ways to incorporate recognition into your existing routines.

One effective approach is to start small within your current practices. Ask yourself what you're already doing consistently, whether it's during monthly team meetings, annual appeals, or regular messages to staff, and find ways to add a line or two to recognize someone's efforts. For example, you might ask your executive leadership team questions like "Who on our team is doing an exceptional job?" or "Who should I have lunch or coffee with this week to better understand their contributions?"

These small shifts can make a significant difference without requiring a complete overhaul of your current methods. Incremental adjustments are manageable and don't feel so overwhelming. Focus on incremental improvements and build good habits. As James Clear writes in *Atomic Habits*,

> Habits are the compound interest of self-improvement. The same way that money multiplies through compound interest, the effects of your habits multiply as you repeat them. They seem to make little difference on any given day and yet the impact they deliver over the months and years can be enormous. It is only when looking back two, five, or perhaps ten years later that the value of good habits and the cost of bad ones becomes strikingly apparent.[28]

Case in point: As I write this, I'm currently on a weight-loss journey. Initially, I was not looking forward to exercising or eating healthily. The process felt so overwhelming, and I thought there was no way I had enough time to eat perfectly and be in the gym for three hours every day.

But I hired a nutritionist, and rather than guilt me into making a total life overhaul, he advised me to make small changes. Changes like swapping white crackers for healthier options or increasing my protein intake. This didn't result in a transformed body overnight, but it did move me closer to my goal. Some suggestions fell by the wayside, like replacing the cream in my morning coffee with a flavored protein shake, but other ideas, like smaller meals multiple times during the day, have stuck. As a result, I've lost over forty pounds in the past year.

Another example: In my early days of ministry, I believed that giving a 10 percent tithe to the church was the only benchmark for commitment. I thought those who didn't meet this standard weren't

---

28 James Clear, *Atomic Habits: An Easy & Proven Way to Build Good Habits & Break Bad Ones* (Penguin Publishing Group, 2018), 16

fully committed. Over time, I understood that people are clear on the five w's: the who, what, where, when, and why of tithing, but little attention is paid to the *how*. Some people want to give more but cannot see how they have the space in their budget to do so. I learned to celebrate those who give 3, 4, or 6 percent, encouraging them to gradually increase their contributions to reach 10 percent or more.

I discovered it's about recognizing and appreciating every step forward, no matter how small. For example, if a few members decide to make small lifestyle changes, like investing in a coffee maker rather than stopping at their local coffee shop or buying groceries in bulk to save money, they can collectively make a significant impact over time. These small, consistent actions can free up resources for important causes, such as supporting the church or helping members in need.

There are many ways you can put this "one bite at a time" principle into action. If you're a manager, having regular check-ins with your staff to ask how they're doing or what they're proud of can uncover insights that you wouldn't otherwise know. Simple questions like "What is something you're proud of this week?" can open doors to deeper connections and understanding.

Again, the key is to focus on making incremental changes that collectively lead to meaningful progress. As the Rev. Dr. Martin Luther King Jr. observed, "If you can't fly then run, if you can't run then walk, if you can't walk then crawl, but whatever you do you have to keep moving forward."

REMEMBER: GET TO KNOW THOSE YOU LEAD

When it comes to getting to know those you lead, consistency is where it's at. As the former publisher of *Success* magazine, Darren Hardy, writes, "It's not the big things that add up in the end. It's the hundreds, thousands, or millions of little things that separate the ordinary from the extraordinary."[29]

When you're a leader who consistently strives to get to know your people, trust me—they will notice. This consistency helps build a culture where everyone feels seen and appreciated, fostering a positive and supportive work environment. It's not about grand gestures every time; even small, regular acknowledgments can make a significant impact.

In *A Long Obedience in the Same Direction,* Eugene H. Peterson wrote that one of the damaging beliefs many people hold on to is "the assumption that anything worthwhile can be acquired at once." He adds, "We assume that if something can be done at all, it can be done quickly and efficiently."[30] But as we know, this is seldom the case. Instead, it's much better to be consistently present in people's lives for years on end.

As John C. Maxwell writes, "Small disciplines repeated with consistency everyday lead to great achievements gained slowly over time."[31] This is something the COVID-19 pandemic emphasized for many church leaders. It taught us that ministry must continue even when life changes and we can't gather in person.

---

29 Darren Hardy, *The Compound Effect: Jumpstart Your Income, Your Life, Your Success,* 10th Anniversary ed. (Hachette Books), 40.

30 Eugene H. Peterson, *A Long Obedience in the Same Direction: Discipleship in an Instant Society* (VP Books), loc. 200, Kindle.

31 John C. Maxwell, *The 15 Invaluable Laws of Growth: Live Them and Reach Your Potential* (Hachette UK, 2012), 74.

During the pandemic, I participated in workshops where pastors shared how they adapted by writing letters to church members or finding other ways to stay connected. They recognized that ministry was not a sprint to be the most popular or innovative. It was a marathon focused on people's lives and their everyday experiences. Their goal was to support their congregations through their highs and lows, demonstrating that God is always present, whether they are at the peak of their happiness or in the depths of despair.

Ultimately, the first step in getting to know those we lead starts with us. As Mahatma Gandhi said, "If you want to change the world, start with yourself."

In both my personal life and my professional role as a CEO, I strive to embrace my unique qualities rather than merely imitating others. Each of us has distinct gifts and perspectives that God has given us, and it's crucial to bring those to the table. By being the best version of ourselves, we not only fulfill our own potential but also contribute uniquely to our organizations and communities.

BULLETIN NOTES

KEY TAKEAWAYS:

- ☑ Trust and effective leadership emerge from truly understanding and valuing the unique stories and aspirations of those you lead.
- ☑ Genuine recognition, even in small doses, can transform individual morale and collective team dynamics.
- ☑ Authentic leadership thrives when leaders embrace their uniqueness while adapting to the diverse needs of their people.

☑ Consistent, incremental actions build a culture of lasting impact, proving that small, thoughtful steps matter more than grand gestures.

KEY QUESTIONS:

1. How can leaders effectively balance their personal leadership style with the need to adapt to the diverse needs of their team or community?
2. In what ways can organizations implement practical and sustainable methods of recognition that go beyond surface-level gestures?
3. How can leaders foster trust in environments where they are perceived as outsiders or face resistance from long-standing team dynamics?

PRINCIPLE 5

Budget Conservatively and Cast Vision Generously

I will give you my message in the form of a vision. Write it clearly enough to be read at a glance ... It may take a long time, but keep on waiting, for it will happen!

—HABAKKUK 2:2–3 (CEV TRANSLATION)

Perhaps when you read the title of this chapter, you did a double take. After all, balancing conservative budgeting with generous vision-casting might seem like trying to mix oil and water. But I can assure you they are a recipe for lasting success.

Budgeting conservatively is about being smart and disciplined with resources. It means taking a clear-eyed look at what you have, what you need, and what's truly worth spending on. In the words of President Barack Obama, "A budget is more than just a series of numbers on a page; it is an embodiment of our values."[32]

Effective budgeting is not just about cutting back or playing it safe. It's about making intentional choices today that set you up for

32 Barack Obama, "Remarks at the American Legion Legislative Rally," *ObamaSpeeches.com*, accessed December 2, 2024, http://obamaspeeches.com/007-American-Legion-Legislative-Rally-Obama-Speech.htm.

stability and growth tomorrow. It's the kind of thinking that ensures you're prepared for unexpected challenges without losing sight of your priorities.

On the other hand, casting a generous vision is what sparks excitement and motivation. It's about dreaming big and inspiring others to believe in what's possible. In *Visioneering*, Andy Stanley writes, "A clear vision, along with the courage to follow through, dramatically increases your chances of coming to the end of your life, looking back with a deep abiding satisfaction, and thinking, I did it. I succeeded. I finished well. My life counted."[33]

Vision gives purpose to the careful planning that budgeting requires. Without a compelling vision, even the most meticulous budget can feel restrictive and uninspiring. But with vision, every dollar spent or saved becomes part of a larger story, one that energizes people to work toward something meaningful.

The magic happens when you combine these two principles. Conservative budgeting keeps you grounded, while generous vision-casting lifts you up. Together, they help you dream responsibly and act boldly.

NAVIGATING THE UNCHARTED GLOBAL PANDEMIC WATERS

When the COVID-19 pandemic hit, almost every business leader struggled to juggle this tension between budgeting and vision-casting. I was still the CEO of Frederick Douglass Charter Public Schools, and I was navigating some uncharted waters. Our nation was scrambling

33 Andy Stanley, *Visioneering: Your Guide for Discovering and Maintaining Personal Vision* (New York: Random House Publishing Group, n.d.), 8–9.

to stay afloat, and the urgency to provide resources for students to study from home became paramount.

I vividly remember those early days in March 2020, sitting with the executive team and debating how to respond. It started with deciding to close schools for just a week. We thought this might give us some breathing room and time to assess and plan. But to me, the superintendent for Frederick Douglass who was technically overseeing three separate charter school districts, the weight of that decision felt enormous.

I remember the whirlwind of communication. This included drafting messages for families, coordinating with staff, and even stepping out of a statewide call with district leaders and the commissioner of education to personally deliver coffee and doughnuts to staff at our New Bedford site. Of course, that one-week closure quickly spiraled into weeks, months, and then the remainder of the school year. The uncertainty was unlike anything we'd ever faced, and the initial scramble was intense.

We needed to ensure every student had access to learning, and that meant getting Chromebooks into their hands as fast as possible. But it wasn't just about technology. We also had to consider formulating lesson plans, printing materials, and even mailing out packets to families. This had its own set of unexpected challenges. Some addresses were inaccurate, and there were students who lived with relatives temporarily due to the pandemic.

Thankfully, at the national level, funding came as a lifeline. Congress passed rounds of Elementary and Secondary School Emergency Relief (ESSER) funds to help schools maintain operations and continue learning. This was critical because it wasn't just about keeping teachers employed. It was also about paying bus drivers, cafeteria staff, and others who suddenly found their roles disrupted. Also, many of our students relied on the school for meals.

With this funding, we faced critical decisions about where to invest. For some districts, the immediate priority was raising teacher salaries and/or hiring more staff. While these investments would have been understandable, we saw the risks. Increasing salaries raised baseline costs, creating a fiscal cliff, a budget shortfall looming once those federal funds dried up. Instead, we chose a different path. Focusing on long-term sustainability, we directed funds toward facility improvements.

The pandemic exposed how ill-suited many schools were for a world where social distancing and ventilation mattered. Schools aren't built to accommodate six feet of distance between students. The federal government's guidance made it clear that space should never again be a barrier to bringing students back to school, so we saw this as an opportunity to expand our existing facilities.

We'd already done a feasibility study before the pandemic, exploring ways to add space to our Boston campus. With the influx of funds, we could accelerate that vision. The goal wasn't just more space. It was creating a better environment for students and staff. We envisioned breakout rooms for one-on-one meetings, upgraded teacher areas, and a college-preparatory look and feel. Through these steps, we hoped to position the school to be a leader in the future.

One of the challenges was selling this vision to both the board and the teachers' union. The union understandably wanted funds directed toward immediate benefits for staff, but we argued that investing in facilities was also an investment in them that created better workspaces and a competitive edge for the school. This was crucial in an environment where strong academic results and robust philanthropy were harder to achieve.

Our ultimate vision extended beyond the pandemic. We imagined building a state-of-the-art STEM lab, attracting partnerships with local biotech firms, and creating a space that could draw students and families by offering something no other charter high school could. We didn't just want to *survive*. We wanted to *thrive* and reimagine what Frederick Douglass could be.

Though I left before the project came to fruition, I take pride in the path we chose. It wasn't the easiest or the most immediately popular, but it was strategic. We avoided the fiscal cliff, built a foundation for the future, and positioned the school to come out of the pandemic stronger. It's a lesson in the power of long-term thinking, even in the face of overwhelming short-term challenges.

KEY TAKEAWAYS WHEN NAVIGATING A CRISIS

There were several key takeaways I took from this time. The first was the need to balance *immediate* needs with *long-term* goals. It's tempting to chase after the shiny urgent solutions right in front of you, but you must keep sight of the bigger picture. The end goal for my leadership team was sustainability and ensuring Frederick Douglass would be a viable charter school option for students long after the pandemic passed. This meant making strategic decisions about how to use resources like the ESSER funds to address immediate needs while also solving long-term challenges.

By choosing to expand our facilities, we solved current issues, such as accommodating social distancing, and addressed future needs, such as making our school more attractive to students and families. It was about creating a lasting impact.

The second principle was managing expectations. In a crisis, everyone has opinions and demands. For us, this included the Boston Teachers Union working through the American Federation of Teachers, the Massachusetts commissioner of education, and even the mayors of Boston and New Bedford. Each had specific visions for what schools should do during the pandemic. At the same time, we were navigating strict deadlines for drawing down ESSER funds, meeting compliance requirements, and ensuring reimbursement processes were followed.

To manage this, we focused on clear, consistent communication. I remember making the decision early on to update families, staff, and the board of directors twice a week, every Monday and Thursday at 4:00 p.m. During this time, I shared everything my team knew. I shared what was happening, what actions were being taken, and what parents or staff needed to do. It was a way to create stability amid chaos, showing our various stakeholders that they could count on consistent information even in unsettling times.

The third principle was seizing the opportunity to rethink and reimagine what was possible. In the words of former White House chief of staff Rahm Emanuel, who himself borrowed the phrase from British statesman Winston Churchill, "Never let a good crisis go to waste." No crisis is good, but many lessons can be learned.

While no one could have anticipated the pandemic, it presented a chance to challenge entrenched systems like the traditional school calendar, which still operates on an outdated agrarian schedule. Historically, American students like my father, a second-generation sharecropper in rural Mississippi, had summers off to help with farming and returned in the fall after the harvest had been reaped. Now, this practice is largely unnecessary. Because of the pandemic, the ideas of year-round schooling, summer remediation programs, or even summer school for all students gained traction as we considered how to recover lost learning time.

But America's infrastructure wasn't ready for this shift. I remember reading about schools closing in August or early September because of inadequate air-conditioning and reflecting on how many schools still lack the basics needed for a year-round model. Even today, schools like those in New York City struggle with antiquated buildings and insufficient cooling systems. The pandemic highlighted these gaps and presented an opportunity to envision a modernized education system.

Of course, systemic challenges always complicate change. At the table with unions, we repeatedly heard phrases like "That's not part of our agreement" or "We'll need concessions for that." These barriers reflect deeper issues in how education is structured and negotiated. But I believe crises like COVID-19 give us the push we need to rethink everything—from calendars to infrastructure—and begin building a system that serves students better in a rapidly changing world.

A GREAT VISION OUTLASTS YOU

One of the challenging and exciting parts of vision-casting is that great visions outlast the one who speaks them into existence. Speaking to the believers at Corinth about the appropriate person to attribute adulation, the apostle Paul says that it is neither he nor his colleague in ministry, Apollos, who deserves praise. As 1 Corinthians 3:6 says, "I planted, Apollos watered, but God gave the increase." Great leaders, like Paul and Apollos, recognize that their role in an organization is temporary and that their job is to hand the ball to someone else.

From a pastor's perspective, my job sometimes involves watering, and sometimes it involves planting, but I also must leave the results up to God. Early on, I accepted the reality that I might never sit under the shade of the trees I've planted or taste the fruit of the seeds I've sown. Yet knowing the tree will grow and provide for others long after I've moved on is enough. It *has* to be enough, or the disappointments would be too heavy to bear.

When I think about the visions I had for previous churches I pastored or organizations I've led, it still stings to think about what could have been accomplished if only I had been reassigned to those churches for a longer tenure. How many more lives could have been changed? What would the impact of bringing these visions to fruition have been for the congregation and communities, respectively? But I remind myself that I'm only responsible for where I am now. This understanding requires humility, and it helps keep my pride in check.

As a pastor or CEO, I am a steward of what God has given me. The vision doesn't belong to me; it belongs to God. If the vision doesn't come to fruition, it doesn't mean the vision was wrong. It simply means either the timing or the place wasn't right.

Not every vision will come to pass immediately—or even in your lifetime. That doesn't mean the vision was wrong. God has a way of planting glimpses of the future in our hearts, but we must trust him to bring them to fruition in his time. Sometimes we're only called to prepare the soil, to plant the seeds, or to water what others have already planted.

The parable of the Sower of the Seed (see Matthew 13:1–13) reminds us that not every seed will fall on good soil. Some will wither, some will be snatched away, and some will flourish. But it only takes a portion to create abundance. That's the hope I cling to when I reflect on the visions I've cast that haven't yet blossomed.

At Bethel AME Church in New Bedford, I envisioned revitalized facilities, community housing, and a church poised for its bicentennial. The plans didn't materialize, but the seeds were planted. Years later, I returned in 2019 to preach a funeral and saw the faded posters still hanging on the walls. Members told me, "We still talk about this from time to time." Those conversations are the echoes of seeds taking root. Even though the vision wasn't realized, its impact remains.

The same applies to my time as pastor of People's Institutional AME Church in Brooklyn, where I imagined turning an empty lot into a resource that could fund ministry for years to come and respond to the changing needs of the largest borough in New York City. It didn't happen while I was there, but I believe the right moment and the right leader will bring that vision or one inspired by it to life.

Great visions always outlast great leaders. They're just too grand. As Pastor Steven Furtick writes, "If the size of your vision for your life isn't intimidating to you, there's a good chance it's insulting to God."[34]

KEEP VISION GROUNDED IN REALITY

That said, a strong vision requires both inspiration and realism. One of the most practical lessons I've learned is to ensure your *vision* is paired with the *provision* to support it. In *Rich Church, Poor Church*, Clif Christopher critiques the "If you build it, they will come" mentality and writes,

> One of the huge mistakes that Poor Churches make is believing that those who will come into the church after it is constructed will be the ones who will pay off the balance owed. The misguided movie quote "Build it and they will come" is on the tombstone of many a church throughout the land. The Rich Church makes all its plans with the understanding that those who are presently making the decision are the ones who will see it through.[35]

Vision is vital, but it must align with the resources and infrastructure you already have or can realistically build. It's better to create a

34 Steven Furtick, *Sun Stand Still: What Happens When You Dare to Ask God for the Impossible* (New York: Crown Publishing Group, 2010), 7.

35 J. Clif Christopher, *Rich Church, Poor Church: Keys to Effective Financial Ministry* (Nashville: Abingdon Press, 2012), 39–40.

space that fills to capacity and requires you to expand or have multiple services than to construct something too large and watch it remain half-empty. Pastor Wayne Cordeiro writes, "It's a gift to be able to launch an inspiring vision. But unless you manage it along the way, it can turn on you, and soon the voracious appetite of the vision consumes you."[36]

A vision that is outpaced by resources isn't just a financial burden; it can also demoralize the people invested in it. If they give and work toward something that feels unattainable, it diminishes their trust in leadership. By budgeting conservatively, you give your vision a solid foundation. By casting vision generously, you ignite passion in people to see what could be and inspire them to take ownership of it.

When a vision is shared with authenticity and passion, it sparks excitement. That excitement is contagious. Whether in a church or a workplace, people are drawn to energy and purpose. As Jim Collins notes, "Great vision without great people is irrelevant."[37]

When people catch the vision, they don't just participate—they invest. They tell their friends, bring their families, and spread the word because they believe in what's being built. There's no greater testament to the strength of a vision than someone saying, "I believe in this so much, I want others to be part of it."

YOUR IDEAS CAN FLOURISH BEYOND YOUR REACH

My journey in the ministry has often involved moving from one place to the next, typically every two years. The itinerary is a core tenet of

36 Wayne Cordeiro, *Leading on Empty: Refilling Your Tank and Renewing Your Passion* (Minneapolis: Bethany House, 2009), 21.

37 Jim Collins, *Good to Great: Why Some Companies Make the Leap ... And Others Don't* (New York: HarperCollins, 2011), 42.

Methodist polity. For bishops, the goal is to match the gifts and graces of the pastor with the ministry needs of a particular congregation. As a result, if you do a good job at one church, you're typically reassigned to one where your gifts and graces can have a greater impact. I've felt the full weight of the pros and cons of this approach.

On the one hand, it's discouraging to leave just when you think things are turning around and headed in the right direction. But on the other, it's exciting to see how places I used to pastor are continuing to grow.

For example, in 2017 at Bethel, I believed that we should celebrate our girls ages five to eighteen in a meaningful way as part of our Women's Season. Why girls? First, I knew if we could get the girls excited, their mothers would follow. And if the girls and their mothers came, the boys would get jealous, creating an opportunity to engage them as well. More importantly, I thought about Malcolm X's words: "The most disrespected person in America is the black woman." I believed that if we could instill pride in our girls early on, we'd give them a foundation to grow and thrive.

Churches, particularly in our denomination, often struggle to maintain active young adult ministries. And who are young adults? They're typically the ones raising children. If we want young adults in church, we need programs that engage their kids—something meaningful enough that parents feel confident and comfortable being involved themselves. At that time, we didn't have many children at Bethel, so I saw this as an opportunity to invite the community and build connections.

The plan was to hold this event, which we later called Black Girl Magic, in September 2017. But as fate would have it, I was reassigned in June of that year to People's Institutional in Brooklyn. Still, I brought the vision with me, and with the blessing of People's Women's

Season Planning Committee, we hosted the first Black Girl Magic event that September—on the same day as Bethel–New Bedford hosted theirs. People's event was small, maybe fifty participants, and a lot was pulled together between July and September. But it was a start, and I was proud of what we accomplished.

By 2018, we had leveled up. Partnering with the local Alpha Kappa Alpha (AKA) sorority chapter was transformative. For context, the AKAs, the first Black sorority founded at Howard University, along with the other panhellenic members of the "Divine 9" sororities and fraternities, hold an influential place in the Black community. Having their resources and energy brought the event to life in ways I couldn't have imagined. That year, we had over two hundred participants. We brought in a professional photographer, featured speakers like our state assemblyperson, addressed critical topics like sex trafficking, and even had the AKAs perform a step show. The event buzzed with excitement, and the high school gym we used was filled with energy and pride.

Now, hosting such an event wasn't cheap. The venue alone cost $900, which felt like a significant investment for our church, to say nothing of the cost of the food, honorariums, supplies, and marketing. I remember hearing concerns like "How will we pay for this? We have bills." But I believed this was about investing in our future. As always, I put my money where my mouth was, writing a personal check to kick-start the effort. Others followed suit, and we raised what we needed—not just for the venue but to cover speaker costs, hotel stays, and even a donation to a South African school for girls.

The impact was immediate. That Sunday, state assemblywoman Tremaine S. Wright, who had spoken at the event, was sitting in the pews. Families who'd attended on Saturday came to church the next day. It was a beautiful moment of connection between the church and the community. Plus, our US senator, Kirsten Gillibrand, later sent a letter congratulating us on meeting a crucial need in our community—a communiqué I read before that morning's offering as a reminder of how financial giving was making a tangible difference.

In 2019, I was assigned to a new church, and my successor didn't carry forward the same vision. But something incredible happened, and that local AKA chapter, whose president was a member of People's, adopted Black Girl Magic as their own. Today, it's still going strong under their leadership, and they've continued to make it a powerful event in the community.

The broader principle I learned is this: when you cast a vision and share it passionately, you create a spark that can ignite lasting change, even if you're not the one to see it through. People are drawn to energy and purpose. When they see you investing in something meaningful, when they see your enthusiasm and commitment, they want to be part of it too.

That's the essence of Black Girl Magic. It wasn't just an event; it was a statement about the value of young Black girls, their potential, and their place in the community. It brought leaders and families into the fold, creating a ripple effect of pride and support that continues today. Whether it's an elected leader showing up or a sorority carrying the torch, it's proof that doing the work matters and that when you plant seeds, they can flourish far beyond your reach.

STILL THERE

I think of another example during my time at Bethel–New Bedford from 2015 to 2017. This church, founded in 1822, shared a story not unlike Mother Emanuel AME Church in Charleston, South Carolina, where the Emmanuel Nine tragically lost their lives. Both churches endured fires and trials but stood resilient as cornerstones of their communities.

Bethel was the only AME church in New Bedford, and I saw its potential to do more to be more. As I looked ahead to its two hundredth anniversary in 2022, I urged the congregation to think big. I told them, "You can't expect people to celebrate 200 years if you don't make 193, 194, and 195 count."

By the church's anniversary in 2017, I unveiled Vision 2022, a revitalization plan that I hoped would transform Bethel for its bicentennial. The plan encompassed much-needed updates to the building that included expanded bathroom facilities, modernized electrical systems, and handicap-accessible office spaces.

We had already upgraded the sound system and recarpeted the sanctuary, but there was so much more to do. The church still ran on knob-and-tube wiring, and the paint was peeling. We even commissioned a feasibility study to determine how to make it all happen. The vision wasn't just about aesthetics. It was about creating a welcoming, functional space for worship and community.

That Sunday, I presented the plan with brochures and posters. The congregation was energized, clapping and cheering by the end of the service. Even the feasibility study consultant attended and vouched for the plan's feasibility. People could see it: a revitalized Bethel, ready for its next century of ministry.

But I didn't stop there. I proposed acquiring two vacant buildings in New Bedford, one diagonally across the street from the church. The idea was to turn them into transitional housing for people in need. I envisioned them as Bethel Manor East and Bethel Manor West, generating income for the church while serving the community. One of the buildings had ample parking space that the church could use, and I walked through the properties multiple times, even bringing our presiding elder to share the vision.

We printed posters of the plan and hung them in the hallway for everyone to see. But in June 2017, when I was reassigned, the plan didn't move forward. The next pastors didn't take up the mantle, and the opportunity to purchase those buildings passed. In 2023, the YWCA acquired one of them, turning it into Drayton House. Yvonne Drayton, the "eponym extraordinaire," as I addressed her on her congratulations card, was a Bethel member who had been a longtime leader at the YWCA. While it's a beautiful testament to what God can do, I still think that could've been Bethel's vision.

Years later, in 2024 I attended a funeral at Bethel, and those posters I'd put up in 2017 were still on the wall—faded and yellowing, but there. A church member told me they still discuss the plan from time to time, and it struck me that even when the work doesn't come to fruition, the seeds planted through a shared vision can linger, inspiring conversations and dreams long after.

My uncle, the Rev. Dr. Johnny W. Poole, a minister in the CME Church, once told me something that resonated deeply. "Kevin," he said, "you can have a vision, but the next pastor after you might not share it. Don't be so tied to the vision that you're disappointed if it doesn't come to pass. Be thankful God gave you the vision and let that be enough."

That wisdom helped me let go of the disappointment, though the experience taught me a valuable lesson. Casting a vision is an act of faith. It's not about control or certainty; it's about trusting that the seeds you plant will grow, even if it's in ways you never anticipated.

I know that each time I return to Bethel, I'm received with open arms. The bond we built, the shared dreams, and the work we started together left an indelible mark. But I've also learned that my role is to cast the vision, do the work, and leave the rest in God's hands. Sometimes, that's all we can do, and it's enough.

REMEMBER: BUDGET CONSERVATIVELY AND CAST VISION GENEROUSLY

Budgeting conservatively while casting vision generously is a delicate but powerful balance. To succeed, you must inspire people to believe in what you're offering. Vision is not simply a plan; it's a story of possibility, a picture of what could be.

People are drawn to purpose, and when they sense authenticity and passion behind a vision, they naturally want to be part of it. Whether you serve in a church, a business, or a community organization, your ability to communicate a compelling vision can be the difference between a fleeting idea and a movement. By focusing on clarity and excitement, you create space for others to imagine themselves within that story. Their belief transforms your vision from a personal dream into a shared mission.

A wide vision requires buy-in from your team. No leader can accomplish significant change alone. Casting a vision broadly is not about dictating a plan but inviting others into it. When you seek input, encourage collaboration, and genuinely listen, you create ownership among your team or community. As John Maxwell observed, a leader without followers is only a person "taking a walk."[38]

People are far more likely to invest their time, resources, and creativity in something they feel they've helped shape. This buy-in isn't just logistical—it's emotional. It builds a culture of shared responsibility, where everyone contributes to the work because they see themselves as part of the story. In Swahili, the word is *ujima*: collective

---

38 "He Who Thinks He Leads but Has No Followers Is Only Taking a Walk," Goodreads, accessed February 26, 2025, https://www.goodreads.com/quotes/479285-he-who-thinks-he-leads-but-has-no-followers-is.

work and responsibility. A vision cast widely becomes a vision carried collectively, which is ultimately far more sustainable.

At the same time, leaders must allow room for their visions to take shape over time. Great visions aren't rigid. They evolve as circumstances change and as new insights emerge. A successful leader understands that the initial idea is a starting point, not a final destination.

When you budget conservatively, you create flexibility—resources that can be redirected or expanded as the vision grows. This room for adaptation ensures that the vision remains viable, even when faced with unexpected challenges. It also allows others to bring their creativity and expertise into the process, making the vision stronger and more comprehensive.

The key to budgeting conservatively and casting vision generously is rooted in trust. Trust in the people you're leading, trust in the process of growth, and trust that the resources you've carefully managed will support the vision when the time comes. A thoughtfully budgeted plan ensures that the vision is not only inspiring but achievable.

At the same time, a generous vision reminds everyone involved that they're working toward something meaningful, something worth striving for. When you marry practicality with imagination, you create an environment where people are inspired to give their best and where the seeds of the vision can take root and flourish.

BULLETIN NOTES

KEY TAKEAWAYS:

- ☑ Balancing conservative budgeting with generous vision-casting combines financial stability with motivational purpose.
- ☑ Addressing immediate needs while prioritizing long-term goals ensures sustainability during crises.
- ☑ Clear, consistent communication fosters trust and aligns stakeholders with a shared vision.
- ☑ A well-cast vision outlasts its originator, inspiring lasting impact beyond the leader's tenure.

KEY QUESTIONS:

1. How can a leader effectively balance the tension between conservative budgeting and the need to inspire others with a generous vision?
2. What steps can be taken to ensure that a vision remains adaptable and sustainable when faced with unforeseen challenges, like a global pandemic?
3. How can leaders foster buy-in and shared ownership of a vision among diverse stakeholders, especially when immediate benefits may not align with long-term goals?

PRINCIPLE 6

Trust but Verify

The best way to find out if you can trust somebody is to trust them.

—ERNEST HEMINGWAY

Trust is the foundation of any strong relationship. It creates an environment where team members feel confident in each other's intentions and commitments. As Simon Sinek writes, "A team is not a group of people that work together. A team is a group of people that trust each other."[39]

However, trust alone isn't always enough to safeguard against misunderstandings, missteps, or intentional deception. This is where the principle of "trust but verify" comes into play. Verifying doesn't undermine trust. It strengthens it by ensuring that actions align with promises.

The phrase "trust but verify" comes from a Russian proverb that became widely known in the West when Ronald Reagan served as president of the United States. Reagan adopted this phrase after being introduced to it by Suzanne Massie, an American writer and expert on

39 Simon Sinek, "A team is not a group of people that work together. A team is a group of people that trust each other," *X* (formerly Twitter), November 17, 2014, https://x.com/simonsinek/status/534495244847689728.

Russian culture who served as an informal advisor on Soviet-American relations. As a result, not only did this phrase become a hallmark of his foreign policy rhetoric, but it became a popular American saying, and it's one I use often.

In business, partnerships thrive when there's mutual trust, but even the best intentions can lead to mistakes or oversights without proper checks in place. Tools like audits and performance reviews help ensure that teams, vendors, and partners are staying on track and meeting their commitments. Similarly, in church leadership, it's important to trust your team to handle their responsibilities while also using systems to monitor progress.

Trust is good, but it's always critical to verify.

PUT IT ON PAPER

As a pastor who has stepped into many new roles, I've realized how important it is to trust *and* verify. Many times, church leaders make the mistake that because they're doing the "Lord's work," everything will just work itself out. Because "God has everything under control," they assume they'll receive adequate compensation, and they don't have to worry about getting anything in writing.

But as I've discovered, this is not the case. This is why I'm a strong advocate of putting everything on paper. Promises are good, trust is important, but paper provides accountability. For example, in June 2017, I was assigned to People's Institutional AME Church in Brooklyn. It was a promotion in terms of responsibility, and it came with the promise of greater resources to facilitate impactful work.

From what I was told to expect, everything seemed like a step forward, and my trust levels were high. To top it all off, the parsonage was described as a spacious, recently renovated seventeen-room house.

But upon arrival, I found the reality was far from what had been presented. Not only was the parsonage in a state of severe disrepair; it was also entirely uninhabitable.

This discovery set off a cascade of challenges. As the denomination's *Doctrine and Discipline* outlined, I had thirty days to vacate my current parsonage in New Bedford to make room for the incoming pastor. This left me scrambling to figure out what to do.

After more communication, I discovered the trustees of People's who were responsible for maintaining the church's property hadn't entered the house in years. Their reasoning was that the previous pastor hadn't allowed access. While I understood their hesitation, I also reminded them that the parsonage, though a pastor's temporary residence, remained the church's house and, therefore, was church property. It was their *duty* to oversee its upkeep. Instead, they'd opted for trust without verification.

Faced with no viable housing, I had to extend my stay in New Bedford's parsonage, negotiate storage for my belongings, and begin commuting between Massachusetts and Brooklyn. My weekends were spent in Brooklyn, staying in hotels, working with the church on Saturdays, leading services on Sundays, and conducting Bible study on Monday nights before driving back to Massachusetts to continue my day job during the week.

This arrangement was far from ideal, but it allowed me to maintain a semblance of continuity in my ministry while the parsonage situation remained unresolved. The costs, however, quickly became overwhelming. Hotels, storage, and extended rental payments all added up. The initial estimates to repair the parsonage began at $100,000 but rapidly escalated as more issues were uncovered. Cracks in the foundation, extensive structural damage, and years of deferred maintenance meant the repair bill ballooned to over $400,000.

After analyzing multiple recommendation charts, we realized that selling the parsonage was the only viable solution of dozens we'd considered, but even that proved a monumental challenge. The sale required approval from the New York attorney general, a legal safeguard in the Empire State meant to protect church assets. Initially, the sale was blocked, leaving us in a financial and logistical quagmire. And things only got worse.

As I dug deeper into the church's affairs, I discovered over $60,000 in citations and liens against the properties. These included unpaid water bills, housing code violations, and other issues that had compounded over the years. In New York, these debts can be sold to private bidders, potentially resulting in the loss of property if left unresolved. Addressing these citations became another urgent priority, adding to the financial pressures on both the church and me.

During this time, I accumulated close to $55,000 in personal debt, covering expenses related to my housing and the church's needs. This weighed heavily on me—not just financially but emotionally and spiritually. I was doing what I believed was right, serving God and the church with all I had, but the lingering fear of what this might cost me was immense.

This is when I decided to act. I couldn't just trust. I had to get it on paper. So, over the next few weeks, I worked with the church leadership to formalize the debt in a promissory note, ensuring that the church recognized and committed to reimbursing me once the parsonage sale was finalized. This was a departure from standard practice but a necessary step to protect both myself and the church's integrity.

Unlike the previous pastor, who had reportedly chosen not to document the debts People's owed to her, I made it a priority to ensure that my financial situation was clear in the church's records. This transparency proved invaluable later when the parsonage was finally sold, allowing me to be fully reimbursed. That moment, while a relief, was bittersweet and a reminder of how close I had come to bearing a permanent financial burden for simply doing my job.

This chapter of my ministry taught me more than I ever wanted to know about the intersection of faith, leadership, and financial responsibility. It reinforced the importance of writing things down, verifying agreements, and advocating for oneself—even in a field as sacred as ministry. As I like to say, "A handshake contract is worth the paper it's printed on."

For anyone stepping into similar roles, my advice is clear: Trust the process but never neglect to verify the details. Document everything, ask questions, and hold people accountable—not out of mistrust but out of respect for the shared mission.

A UNIQUE CHALLENGE FOR PASTORS

When it comes to pastoring, the whole "trust but verify" concept is challenging. In the business world, you have access to tools like corporate credit cards, institutionalized processes, and operational safety nets that can absorb unforeseen expenses. In churches, however, financial management often hinges on tradition, limited resources, and, sometimes, lack of preparedness.

These differences create unique challenges for ministry leaders, especially when they step into a role for which they may not have been adequately trained. To combat this trend, I teach a class in our denomination's Ministerial Institute, which is a four-year program that supplements seminary education for those pursuing ordination. My course is on church administration, and it's one of the few that addresses the practical, often-overlooked aspects of pastoring.

As I share with my students, the reality is that you can be an excellent preacher skilled at delivering God's word but completely unequipped to handle the administrative burdens that come with leading a church. "What happens when you walk into a church and find financial chaos?" I ask them. "What do you do if you're greeted with shutoff notices for utilities on your very first day?"

I can answer these questions with firsthand experience because this is exactly what happened to me when I arrived at People's. While it was jarring, I had the advantage of a background in finance, so I knew how to negotiate with utility companies and stave off the immediate crises. Also, I'd been through similar situations before.

In one of my previous appointments, the churches were already in foreclosure when I arrived. Those experiences prepared me to face utility shutoff notices, but People's came with its own unique complications. For instance, in New York City you can access a website to check for liens on a property. I discovered that one of the church's lots had been turned into an illegal parking lot by a member of the congregation. A complaint had been filed, fines had been issued, and they had gone unpaid for so long that the compounded interest was astronomical. Talk about a headache.

Now, I make it a point to warn my students about these pitfalls, so they're prepared if and/or when they step into similar situations. For many of my students, this is an eye-opener. They often come into the class expecting to learn about leading official board meetings and meeting denominational assessments. As a result, they inevitably initially resist the material I share. But by the end of the course, they often tell me it's the most valuable class they've taken.

This issue is unique to churches in many ways, but at its core, it speaks to leadership and the risks leaders are willing to take to move a vision forward. One of the most critical lessons I've learned and now teach is this: you cannot risk more than you can afford to lose.

FROM BAD TO WORSE

This principle became a stark reality for me during my time at People's. While maintaining my residence in Massachusetts, I sought to balance my dual responsibilities: pastoring People's and fulfilling my role as the COO of Maya Angelou Charter Public Schools. After all, I was responsible for all the non-academic aspects of the commonwealth's largest charter network. This arrangement required significant flexibility and financial support, so I approached my manager, the executive director of Maya Angelou Charter Public Schools, to apprise him of my promotion and outline my needs.

I explained that I would need to work remotely on Mondays to accommodate my commuting schedule, which was an uncommon request in the pre-pandemic era. Additionally, he highlighted the financial burden associated with regular travel and lodging. During this conversation, we verbally agreed that Maya Angelou Charter Public Schools would provide $15,000 annually to cover these costs. While the number seemed clear at the time, we failed to formalize this agreement in writing, a decision that would later prove to be a costly oversight.

Believing this arrangement to be settled but unclear on whether the funds would be paid directly in my paycheck, as a stipend, or otherwise, I used my Maya Angelou–issued credit card to cover expenses for my hotel stays and other costs incurred while fulfilling my pastoral duties in Brooklyn. As the leader of the finance function in the organization, I presumed these charges would be reconciled against the agreed-upon $15,000 at year's end. However, as the months passed, the costs of commuting and lodging mounted, and I found myself exceeding the initial estimate. Despite this, I remained confident that we would resolve any discrepancies amicably.

The situation grew more complex when I accepted the position of CEO at Frederick Douglass in June 2018, necessitating my departure from Maya Angelou Charter Public Schools. During my exit, tensions arose between myself and the executive director. While he had been informed of my planned transition and was supportive of my decision to spread my wings, he was unaware that three other team members—a director of finance, a general counsel, and an administrative assistant—had also decided to leave and join me at Frederick Douglass. Their resignations created operational challenges for Maya Angelou Charter Public Schools, leaving the executive director feeling blindsided and betrayed.

These tensions boiled over when the $15,000 agreement came into question. The executive director asserted that he had only committed to $5,000—a figure starkly different from what I recalled. With no formal documentation to substantiate my claim, the matter escalated to Maya Angelou's board of directors. I was summoned to a meeting where the board chair, the executive director, and other leaders scrutinized the expenses I had incurred. After reviewing the transactions, they concluded that I owed approximately $45,000, despite my insistence that $15,000 of this amount had been verbally agreed upon as a reimbursement.

To address the immediate financial dispute, I wrote a check for roughly $12,000 on the spot and proposed a payment plan for the remaining balance. However, the board also decided to withhold the $15,000 bonus I earned for my work during the year, further compounding the financial strain. For me, this decision felt not only unjust but punitive—a result of personal grievances rather than a fair assessment of the facts.

The fallout didn't stop there. The executive director took the matter to the Massachusetts Charter School Association, where I served as treasurer, alleging financial improprieties. As a result, I was asked to resign from my position—a role I had valued deeply. This series of events not only hurt me professionally but also tarnished my reputation within the charter school community. Although no formal charges were brought against me, the mere suggestion of misconduct was enough to cast a shadow over my contributions.

In reflecting on this experience, I realized that the lack of a written agreement had left me vulnerable to disputes and misunderstandings. What had initially seemed like a straightforward verbal arrangement unraveled into a contentious and deeply personal conflict. The financial and emotional toll was significant. Between September 2018 and February 2019, I worked tirelessly to repay the remaining debt, all while adjusting to my new role at Frederick Douglass and continuing to pastor People's.

Looking back, I realize this ordeal taught me invaluable lessons and certainly strengthened my character. Navigating these challenges, I drew strength from my faith, my family, and my community. I often reflected on the fourth verse of words of one of my favorite hymns, "We're Often Tossed and Driven," which became an anthem during this difficult period. I can't tell you how many times I hummed these lyrics:

Temptations, hidden snares often take us unawares,

And our hearts are made to bleed for
many a thoughtless word or deed,

And we wonder why the test when we try to do our best,

But we'll understand it better by and by.

In hindsight, this chapter of my life was a desert experience. It was unbelievably hard. But through it, I learned many invaluable lessons that have served me well to this day. The most important lesson was to document *everything.*

While trust is an essential foundation for any relationship, it must be paired with concrete agreements to protect all parties involved. Verbal commitments, no matter how sincere, are subject to memory lapses, shifting priorities, and, in some cases, outright revisionist history. As painful as this experience was, it reinforced the necessity of putting everything on paper, even when dealing with colleagues and leaders I respected.

KNOW WHAT YOU'RE WALKING INTO

As a leader, you're inevitably going to step into situations that catch you off guard. These are unavoidable. But rather than just trusting everything you're told, make sure you verify through critical conversations and proper documentation.

I think back to my time at the Carver Center, where I served as CFO and then CFO and interim COO. When I was promoted to interim CEO in December 2022, I stepped into a role previously held by a deeply committed leader who had built the organization but had made sacrifices that complicated the succession process. The outgoing CEO, who didn't have children and was financially secure, had set her salary far below market value.

While her decision came from a place of love for the organization, it created challenges for those who would follow her. I pointed this out during my tenure as CFO, explaining that if we ever needed to replace her, we'd struggle to attract a candidate of her caliber at her current salary. She acknowledged the issue but brushed it aside, confident in her dedication to the mission.

When she stepped down, the board of directors faced the question of what my salary would be. They decided that my salary could not exceed hers, though it was only $10,000 more than what I was making as the CFO and interim COO. Plus, the board did not want to backfill the CFO role but instead wanted me to continue as interim CEO *and* CFO. This struck me as inequitable, given the added workload, direct reports, and increased travel demands. After I raised my concerns, the board chair proposed a compromise. I would receive an additional $7,500 per month for the duration of my interim CEO role.

This seemed like a fair solution, and I agreed with it. However, this is where the principle of "trust but verify" became crucial. One of my colleagues advised me to clarify whether the $7,500 was meant to be paid monthly or at the end of my term. I assumed the arrangement was consistent with my previous bonus structure as CFO and that the payments would come at the end of the interim period. Confident in this understanding, I made plans with my family and financial advisors for how we'd use the funds to offset the added stress and workload I'd taken on.

But the reality didn't unfold as expected. Shortly after the agreement was made, the board chair stepped down due to a breast cancer diagnosis, leaving a leadership vacuum on the board. For months, there was no clear point of contact or managerial oversight while we were converting to nonprofit. When I eventually raised the issue of my bonus with the new board chair, I was told that bonuses were paid only at the end of the calendar year—despite the specific terms in my contract.

By this time, I had served six months as interim CEO and was owed $45,000 in bonuses. But the organization refused to pay, citing their internal policies. Two weeks later, I was let go, and while I received a severance package, it didn't include the promised bonus. Although my attorney was able to increase the size of my severance by two months' worth of pay, she advised that protracted litigation could substantially reduce my claim. This experience was a harsh reminder that even written agreements can fall apart when leadership changes or critical details are overlooked.

The departing board chair hadn't had the chance to fully communicate the reasoning behind the bonus structure, and I was left to bear the consequences. It was a frustrating and disheartening experience, one that left me feeling undervalued despite my sacrifices for the organization. In the end, I had no one to blame but myself because I should have done my due diligence and verified.

REMEMBER: TRUST BUT VERIFY

When navigating professional, organizational, or personal relationships, there are several important principles to remember.

First, never risk more than you can afford to lose. Before committing to any agreement, whether financial, professional, or personal, consider what you're putting on the line and what happens if things don't go as planned. Can you handle the loss of time, money, or effort if it isn't reciprocated? If not, rethink your approach. This principle applies to everything, even something as seemingly simple as vacation time. Take what you're owed. Claim your benefits. When you forgo what is rightfully yours, it doesn't just harm you—it creates systemic imbalances, misrepresenting the true cost of your efforts. Know your value and ensure your contributions are acknowledged.

Next, remember that handshake agreements are never enough. Every agreement, whether it's a formal contract or a casual understanding with a colleague, should be documented. Writing things down provides clarity and accountability, reducing potential misunderstandings. But even written agreements have limitations. Leadership changes, forgetfulness, or deliberate undermining can weaken them over time. That's why it's crucial to revisit and review your agreements periodically, ideally with the help of a third party like an attorney. It's a simple step that can save you significant trouble later.

Regular verification is equally important. Written agreements mean little if they aren't enforced. Take the time to ensure retirement contributions are made, beneficiaries are updated, and insurance policies are current. Trust doesn't eliminate the need for vigilance. It reinforces it.

Plan for the worst while hoping for the best. Death, illness, or unexpected changes often reveal the worst in people. Probate courts exist because of inadequate planning and ambiguous wishes. Writing a will, updating beneficiaries, and communicating your plans clearly can prevent unnecessary disputes and ensure your intentions are honored. This principle applies to organizations too. Leaders often assume that goodwill and trust will suffice, but self-interest and miscommunication frequently get in the way. Document your intentions, secure your rights, and verify regularly to protect yourself.

Finally, recognize that change brings risks. Leadership transitions, whether in businesses or churches, can jeopardize established agreements. New leaders might fail to honor previous commitments, either unintentionally or by prioritizing other goals. Periodic reviews and clear documentation can help mitigate these risks.

By understanding and applying these principles, you can safeguard your future, your relationships, and your peace of mind. Trust is important, but always verify.

BULLETIN NOTES

KEY TAKEAWAYS:

- ☑ Trust is essential for strong relationships, but pairing it with verification strengthens accountability and ensures alignment with commitments.
- ☑ Written agreements provide clarity and protection, highlighting the limitations of verbal promises and handshake deals.
- ☑ Challenges in leadership transitions and financial oversight underscore the necessity of regular verification and due diligence in both professional and personal contexts.
- ☑ Leaders must plan for the worst by documenting agreements and maintaining vigilance to safeguard against unforeseen disputes and changes.

KEY QUESTIONS:

1. How can leaders balance trusting their teams while implementing systems of accountability without undermining trust?
2. What steps should individuals take to ensure verbal agreements are properly formalized to avoid potential disputes?
3. In what ways can organizations and leaders proactively address the risks associated with leadership transitions and changes in agreements?

PRINCIPLE 7

Disagree without Being Disagreeable

Honest disagreement is often a good sign of progress.

—MAHATMA GANDHI

It's no secret we live in polarized times when "a record-high 80% of U.S. adults believe Americans are greatly divided on the most important values."[40]

With the rise of social media and the opportunity to have an opinion on every topic, it's easy to view our friends and acquaintances through the lens of what divides rather than what unites us. Disagreements are an inevitable part of life, whether in personal relationships, workplaces, or public discourse. They arise naturally from the diversity of thought, values, and experiences that define human interactions.

Yet the way we handle disagreements can determine whether they become opportunities for growth or sources of conflict. At its core, disagreeing respectfully requires a commitment to seeing the other

40 Jeffrey M. Jones, "Americans Agree the Nation Is Divided on Key Values," *Gallup News*, September 23, 2024, https://news.gallup.com/poll/650828/americans-agree-nation-divided-key-values.aspx.

person's humanity beyond their opinions. It's not about winning an argument but about engaging in dialogue that seeks common ground.

When we approach disagreements with humility and empathy, we signal that we value the person even if we don't share their perspective. This approach can transform contentious conversations into meaningful exchanges where both parties feel heard and respected. In an era where polarization often dominates discourse, the ability to disagree agreeably has never been more important. It allows us to *challenge ideas* without *attacking individuals*, making it possible to address critical issues without alienating those with opposing views.

By focusing on the issue at hand rather than resorting to personal attacks or dismissive attitudes, we can create environments where creativity, innovation, and mutual understanding thrive. One of the most profound lessons I've learned is the value of looking beyond the initial perceptions of people, especially when those perceptions are colored by competition or skepticism.

What I've found time and again is that those who might initially appear as obstacles or rivals can become some of your most trusted allies, given the right approach and mutual understanding. Here are a few examples.

THREE UNLIKELY ALLIES

When I applied for the CEO role at Frederick Douglass, the application process was intense and drawn out. My first interview was in March, but I didn't hear back for weeks. The committee informed me they were also vetting an internal candidate, which I respected. By the time June rolled around, I found myself presenting at a board meeting, deliberately structured so I wouldn't cross paths with the other candidate. Only later did I learn that the person I had unknowingly competed against was the principal of one of our three schools, someone deeply rooted in the organization and looking to move up to the CEO role.

Her name was Brenda, and her extensive experience within the organization made her a strong candidate. Naturally, my selection for the role left her disappointed, and others in the organization warned me against bringing her into my leadership team. They cited her long tenure, her reputation for being brash at times, and her history of challenging interpersonal relationships. Many advised me to distance myself from her, arguing that her presence might undermine the new administration I was building.

But I took a different view. Brenda came to me shortly after my appointment and expressed her desire to leave her role as principal to join the network office in a leadership capacity. She was willing to work with me and align with the vision I was setting for the organization. In my mind, if someone who had been a competitor was willing to collaborate and take that step, it was worth giving them a chance.

Brenda became a trusted advisor and friend. I didn't make her the chief academic officer, the role she initially sought, but instead I created the position of chief schools officer, where she managed the principals and oversaw the quality and operations of all schools. Her institutional knowledge proved invaluable, as she had been with the organization for nearly two decades, working her way up from a teaching fellow role to leadership positions. She understood the organization's history, culture, and pain points better than anyone else, and her insights became critical as we navigated challenges together.

When I decided to step down from my role at Frederick Douglass, I recommended to the board that Brenda be named my successor without a lengthy search process. I believed deeply that she was the right person to carry the organization forward. In retrospect, turning the baton over to Brenda remains one of the decisions I'm most proud of, because someone who others said should be a foe became my strongest ally.

The second example of discovering an unexpected ally was during my time at the Carver Center. During the interview process for the CFO role, I unknowingly competed against Loretta, another external candidate. After I was selected, the CEO decided to create a role for Loretta as chief people officer, a decision that initially left me skeptical. I wondered if this was someone I could trust, given that she had been vying for the same position I had.

Despite my initial reservations, Loretta and I developed a strong working relationship. When the CEO decided to step down, Loretta and I were the only two people in the organization who knew about it in advance. For two months, we had to carry the weight of this secret while preparing the organization for the transition.

During that time, Loretta became one of my most trusted confidants and friends. She helped me implement strategies, navigate internal politics, and support the organization during a period of uncertainty. Her commitment and partnership were indispensable, and she became someone I could count on completely.

A third critical relationship, this one also at the Carver Center, was with Carol. She was the general manager in Houston and was described by other executive team members as toxic and untrustworthy. Some even pointed to her as the poster child for the challenges at our Texas location. I was repeatedly warned to steer clear of her, but my own interactions told a very different story.

Over time, Carol proved to be not just a reliable ally and trusted thought partner; it became clear why she was the "secret sauce" in the Houston ecosystem who was creating the opportunities that the entire organization benefited from. Moreover, Carol expanded my professional network and championed my place in the industry long after my time at the Carver Center ended. Today, we remain in touch, and her ongoing support continues to open doors for me.

FOUR KEY TAKEAWAYS

These three experiences taught me many important lessons:

1. Do not write people off based on perceptions or past rivalries.
2. Both Brenda and Loretta were initially positioned as competitors or potential obstacles in my career journey. Yet, by engaging with them openly and giving them a chance, I discovered allies who brought immense value to their respective organizations and to me personally.
3. Strong people can be strong voices.
4. Brenda's long tenure at Frederick Douglass gave her a perspective on what had worked in the past and what hadn't. Similarly, Carol's years as the Carver Center's principal fundraiser provided invaluable insights. If I had steered clear of them because of their strong personalities, I would have missed out on the wonderful wisdom they offered.
5. A secure environment is the foundation for healthy disagreement.
6. In *Crucial Conversations*, Kerry Patterson writes, "People rarely become defensive simply because of what you're saying. They only become defensive when they no longer feel safe. The problem is not the content of your message, but the condition of the conversation."[41]

41 Kerry Patterson et al., *Crucial Conversations: Tools for Talking When Stakes Are High*, 2nd ed. (New York: McGraw-Hill, 2011), 55.

7. Know when your organization needs a new voice.

8. Recognizing when to step aside, as I did at Frederick Douglass Charter Public Schools, isn't a sign of weakness. It's a demonstration of strength and confidence in others. By recommending Brenda as my successor, I helped ensure the organization's continuity and success. Likewise, by promoting Carol to chief development and investment officer, I positioned the Carver Center for continued success and growth beyond North America.

In all three experiences, what began as situations of rivalry and skepticism evolved into partnerships that strengthened the organizations and enriched my own growth as a leader. By not allowing healthy disagreement to lead to division, I was able to build a stronger team.

DIVISIVENESS IS EVERYWHERE

Navigating divisiveness, whether in politics, the workplace, or personal relationships, requires a deep commitment to understanding and respect. I often remind myself that some of the people closest to me don't share my political or ideological views. There are people on my Christmas list who didn't vote the way I did, yet our shared bonds—whether rooted in faith, history, or mutual experiences—are stronger than those differences. These connections remind me that common ground is the key to meaningful dialogue, especially during challenging times.

For example, during 2024's contentious election season, I wrote an op-ed in the *Atlanta Journal-Constitution*. A former colleague reached out afterward, questioning how I could support the candidate I did. She cited her list of issues and why I should change my perspective. But rather than get defensive, I shared a personal story with her of how I had arrived at my views. While this didn't change her mind on our areas of disagreement, we remained associates.

She didn't agree, but she thanked me for my candor. That exchange reinforced the idea that we can disagree profoundly and still respect each other. It's about seeing the humanity in someone else and valuing the shared connections that transcend politics or ideology. Conversations like that require a willingness to assume the best intentions in others, even when their views clash with our own. Instead of approaching disagreements with judgment, displaying curiosity and respect can open doors to understanding.

This principle extends to the workplace, where disagreements can easily become personal if we're not careful. When I started at the Carver Center, I noticed a culture where feedback was rare, and grievances went unspoken. Small issues festered, leading to a toxic environment where colleagues undermined each other rather than working collaboratively. One of my priorities was to normalize feedback and encourage open dialogue. I pushed for people to address issues directly and constructively. For example, if someone felt slighted or overlooked, I encouraged them to speak up immediately rather than let resentment grow. This shift wasn't easy, but it was necessary to create a healthier and more functional team dynamic.

Disagreeing constructively also means separating the *person* from the *problem*. Disagreements shouldn't define relationships. They're about addressing specific issues, not attacking individuals. When disagreements are resolved, it's essential to leave them behind and move forward collaboratively.

I call this "disagree and commit," a phrase I first learned at Denmark Vesey. Once a decision is made, everyone involved needs to commit fully to its success, regardless of who originally proposed the idea. As Ray Dalio says, "To be successful, we need everyone to think independently and work through disagreement to decide what's best."[42] If the decision turns out to be wrong, you address it as a team, not as an opportunity for someone to say, "I told you so." This approach builds trust and ensures that disagreements don't undermine collective progress.

At the Carver Center, the absence of this principle was painfully obvious. The executive team didn't like each other, and it showed. Meetings were tense, and unresolved conflicts spilled over into conversations with staff, eroding trust across the organization. People left meetings frustrated, and confidentiality was routinely breached. It was clear that many executives lacked the basic skills to function at an executive level, and the organization suffered as a result. That experience underscored for me how critical it is to foster a culture of respect, accountability, and commitment in any team.

Finding unity in divided times isn't about agreeing on everything; it's about focusing on shared values and the greater good. Ultimately, what matters most is the ability to engage with others in a way that builds bridges rather than walls. Whether it's in a personal relationship, a workplace, or a national debate, the key is to approach conversations with openness, empathy, and a genuine desire to understand. By doing so, we can navigate disagreements constructively, strengthen relationships, and move forward together, even in the most divided of times.

42 Richard Feloni, "Ray Dalio, Head of the World's Largest Hedge Fund, Explains His Succession Plan for Bridgewater and How Its 'Radically Transparent' Culture Is Misunderstood," *Business Insider*, March 21, 2016, https://www.businessinsider.com.

HOW TO CREATE AN AGREEABLE CULTURE

Establishing trust in an organization and creating an environment where people feel comfortable bringing their full selves to the table takes intentionality, time, and often a willingness to be vulnerable. It's a gradual process, but there are practical steps leaders can take to expedite the trust-building process, especially in settings where mistrust or guardedness is the norm.

One approach that has worked well for me is an exercise called multidimensional identities. It involves participants identifying the elements of their identity that are most core to who they are, as well as secondary or peripheral aspects. For example, in my inner circle, I might include being a pastor, a dad, and a Black man. In the outer circles, I might mention being from Michigan or a fan of a particular football team.

This exercise allows individuals to share personal aspects of themselves in a structured way, creating immediate vulnerability and connection. When I first introduce this exercise in an organization or at church, I model it by sharing my own circles, which often surprises people. It gives colleagues and congregants alike a glimpse into parts of me they wouldn't have guessed, breaking down barriers and fostering a sense of community.

Following the multidimensional identities exercise, I've used tools like Kahoot! to deepen those connections in a fun, engaging way. Kahoot! is an online platform I learned about at church where you can create custom quizzes, and I've used it to design questions based on the identities shared during the previous exercise. Questions like "Which staff members have traveling abroad on their bucket list?" or "Who here is a twin or triplet?" prompt playful interactions and moments of discovery, such as colleagues realizing they share unexpected commonalities.

These activities can quickly create a sense of camaraderie, especially for new leaders trying to establish themselves in unfamiliar environments. While they don't replace the need for long-term relationship building, they offer a way to jump-start the process. Modeling vulnerability as a leader is crucial, as it sets the tone and signals that you're invested in getting to know your team and building mutual respect.

Beyond these interactive tools, I've found tremendous value in resources like *The 6 Types of Working Genius* and *The Four Tendencies*. The first book identifies six areas of talent, dividing them into two each of "geniuses," "competencies," and "frustrations." It highlights the importance of ensuring people are working in their zones of genius rather than their zones of frustration. If someone is consistently stuck in tasks that drain them, it can lead to dissatisfaction and conflict. Understanding where people thrive and where they struggle can help leaders assign roles and responsibilities more effectively, reducing friction and boosting morale.[43]

The competitive nature of the game, complete with rankings and small prizes, creates a lively atmosphere where people laugh, cheer, and bond. It's a lighthearted way to reinforce connections and build trust and get to know what others are good at. As author Patrick Lencioni writes in *The 6 Types of Working Genius*, "Teams and organizations that help people tap into their God-given talents are much more successful and productive than those that don't."[44]

The Four Tendencies focuses on how individuals approach expectations, whether internal or external. It identifies four per-

---

43 Richard Feloni, "Ray Dalio, Head of the World's Largest Hedge Fund."

44 Patrick M. Lencioni, *The 6 Types of Working Genius: A Better Way to Understand Your Gifts, Your Frustrations, and Your Team* (Dallas: BenBella Books, 2020), 1.

sonality types: Upholders, Questioners, Obligers, and Rebels. This framework helped me recognize that some people's behaviors in the workplace or at church—like relentless questioning—weren't necessarily personal attacks on my leadership but rather an expression of their natural tendencies. For example, a Questioner isn't doubting you to be combative; they genuinely need answers to feel comfortable moving forward. Rebels, on the other hand, resist being told what to do and need the freedom to make their own choices. Understanding these dynamics can transform how you interact with team members and diffuse tension.[45]

For leaders who may not feel comfortable with more interactive exercises like Kahoot! or multidimensional identities, these books provide an alternative way to build understanding and trust. They offer actionable insights into how people work and how to interact with them more effectively. Whether you're dealing with a Rebel on your team or trying to identify why someone seems perpetually frustrated, these frameworks provide tools to navigate those challenges.

The key takeaway is that trust isn't about forcing people to align perfectly or agree on everything. It's about creating a space where differences are understood and respected. By learning who your people are, what their geniuses are, and what frustrates them, you can foster an environment where feedback is normalized, conflicts are addressed constructively, and everyone feels valued. Trust grows when people see that you're invested in understanding them, not just as employees but as individuals. That's what transforms a guarded, siloed team into a cohesive, collaborative one.

---

45 Author, *The Four Tendencies* (Publisher, year).

REMEMBER: DISAGREE WITHOUT BEING DISAGREEABLE

Disagreeing without being disagreeable requires a commitment to humility, consistency, and a willingness to see beyond the moment of conflict. It's about extending the same grace we'd hope to receive and resisting the urge to let disagreements define relationships. One of the most profound lessons I've learned as a pastor and leader is that relationships are dynamic, and time has a way of shifting perspectives if we remain steadfast in our kindness and integrity.

As a pastor, I've often found myself in situations where the grace I extend isn't reciprocated. Last year, I tried to reform our church's budget process to make it more transparent and inclusive. Instead of having a small group quietly decide on the core elements of the budget, I proposed putting a draft out in May for discussion and questions before the June vote.

What followed was a barrage of lengthy emails from congregants who challenged me and undermined my leadership. It was frustrating, not just because of the work involved but because the effort was veiled in conspiracy. Still, I answered every question, addressed every concern, and met the resistance with persistence and grace.

When confronted with the coordination, some members were defensive and upset. But I didn't let that deter me from treating them with care. If they were sick or discouraged, they received a card as usual. If they experienced loss in their immediate family, the peace lily arrived as always. I continued to extend my hand, even if it wasn't warmly received. Grace, I've learned, is as much about consistency as it is about kindness. It's about treating people the same, regardless of how they treat you, because favoritism or retaliation undermines the integrity of leadership.

Disagreeing with grace is not about being a doormat or avoiding accountability. It's about maintaining your values and integrity while holding others accountable in a way that reflects love and respect. It's about remembering that our disagreements don't define us and that our shared humanity is always greater than our differences. Above all, it's about trusting that grace, when consistently practiced, has the power to transform even the most difficult relationships over time.

BULLETIN NOTES

FOUR KEY TAKEAWAYS:

- ☑ Disagreeing respectfully requires empathy and humility, focusing on the shared humanity of others rather than personal victories in arguments.
- ☑ Constructive disagreements rely on creating a safe environment where individuals feel heard and valued, fostering dialogue and innovation.
- ☑ Viewing rivals or critics as potential allies, as demonstrated through personal experiences, can lead to unexpected partnerships and organizational strength.
- ☑ Building trust and understanding individual differences—whether through vulnerability, structured activities, or personality frameworks—are essential for creating cohesive, collaborative teams.

KEY QUESTIONS:

1. How can leaders effectively cultivate a culture of open dialogue and constructive feedback within highly polarized or guarded environments?

2. What practical steps can organizations take to ensure that disagreements are focused on issues rather than personal attacks?

3. How can leaders consistently extend grace and maintain integrity when their efforts to foster inclusivity and transparency are met with resistance?

PRINCIPLE 8

Personnel Matters Should Not Be Personal

Strong managers who make tough decisions to cut jobs provide the only true job security in today's world. Weak managers are the problem. Weak managers destroy jobs.

—JACK WELCH

The most difficult part of leadership is making tough decisions that you know might hurt those you care about.

In *Crucial Conversations*, Kerry Patterson writes, "The root cause of many—if not most—human problems lies in how people behave when others disagree with them about high-stakes, emotional issues."[46] Whether it's letting someone go, addressing performance issues, or transitioning a team member out of a role, these moments are challenging because they impact people's lives in profound ways.

However, you must learn to navigate these situations with a balance of humanity and professionalism. The key principle is simple: *personnel matters should not be personal.* This doesn't mean you disregard

46 Kerry Patterson, Joseph Grenny, Ron McMillan, and Al Switzler, *Crucial Conversations: Tools for Talking When Stakes Are High*, 2nd ed. (New York: McGraw-Hill, 2012), loc. 239, Kindle.

the humanity of those involved. On the contrary, treating people with dignity and respect is essential. But it does mean separating personal relationships from organizational needs.

As a leader, you must prioritize what's best for the *group*, even when it's uncomfortable or risks damaging personal connections. This clarity ensures your organization remains focused on its mission, unclouded by personal biases or emotional entanglements. In his book *Relational Intelligence*, Dharius Daniels describes achieving this clarity as a critical step toward achieving our God-given purpose.

Great leadership is about balancing empathy with decisiveness. You can still acknowledge the contributions of individuals and celebrate their impact, even while making a choice that might have an immediate negative effect on them. Of course, this is far from easy, and I have my share of scars that have come from business and friendship coming to a head.

WHEN FRIENDSHIPS AND BUSINESS COLLIDE

I think back to my time at Frederick Douglass, where I started with a colleague and close friend of mine. She was someone I had supported through thick and thin, and we had a solid bond. When she joined Frederick Douglass, she took on a dual role as general counsel and chief of staff. Among her many responsibilities, she managed payroll and HR functions, which made sense since we were amid union negotiations. However, this was her first time managing an employee, and it became clear that there were some gaps in her approach.

One of the critical tasks in her role was overseeing the payroll process, including staff-renewal decisions. For charter schools, renewal is the process of determining whether employees will return and informing them about their salaries for the upcoming year. It's a nuanced process, especially since we had both ten-month and twelve-month employees at Frederick Douglass. Unfortunately, when it came time to finalize payroll and budget exercises, she admitted that she had mishandled the designations of certain employees. This mistake ended up costing the organization roughly $60,000.

When she told me about the error, I appreciated her honesty but knew the implications were serious. I had to inform the board chair, and as a leader, I couldn't justify promoting her to COO—a position she had been working toward.

This wasn't an easy decision. I respected her deeply and valued her contributions, but I couldn't overlook the mistake or its impact on the organization. So, I went to her house to talk it over. Sitting at her kitchen table, I explained the situation, the consequences, and why I couldn't recommend her promotion. She was understandably upset. She felt she had been underpaid in her previous role at Maya Angelou and saw the COO position as a step toward fairer compensation and economic freedom. She believed in her potential, and I did too, but I still knew there was no way I could promote her at this time.

I expressed my support for her personally, but I emphasized that I had to draw a line between personal relationships and professional obligations. Later, when we had to close our New Bedford campus and consolidate into a single site in Boston, the organizational structure changed dramatically. Without the network office, her role and many others were eliminated. Once again, I had to sit down with her and, this time, explain that we would pay her through the remainder of the school year but that she had six months to find a new job.

This conversation, like the earlier one, was tough. She was angry and felt like I was playing favorites. As a result, our relationship has never been the same since. Painful as this was, as a leader I believe in making decisions based on the needs of the work, not individual relationships.

When designing an organizational structure, it's crucial to focus on the roles required and then consider the people, not the other way around. Otherwise, you risk undermining the organization's goals. Yes, treat people with respect and care, even during terminations or role changes. These are people with families, responsibilities, and futures. But never lose sight that you are a leader, and sometimes you'll be forced to make decisions that are extremely difficult.

LAY A PROPER GROUNDWORK FOR TOUGH CONVERSATIONS

One of the reasons so many leaders struggle to have difficult conversations is that they've done a very poor job communicating expectations. They dished out empty compliments when they knew their team member's job performance wasn't up to par. Finally, one day they hit a wall and verbally vomit all their complaints at once, leaving the employee stunned.

If you're a strong leader, performance feedback should never come as a surprise to those you lead. If someone gets an end-of-year review or a formal critique and it blindsides them, that's a breakdown in leadership communication. Weekly check-ins or regular feedback sessions should make it clear if someone is falling short of expectations. By the time something is written down or formally addressed, it should already feel familiar to the person. In *Unreasonable Hospitality*, Will Guidara writes, "Whether criticism or praise, it's a leader's job to give their team feedback all the time."[47]

---

47 Will Guidara, *Unreasonable Hospitality: The Remarkable Power of Giving People More Than They Expect* (Penguin Publishing Group), 70.

In both termination and performance-adjustment conversations, preparation is key. Understand that these conversations won't be easy, but approach them with clarity, respect, and a focus on what's best for the organization. By being direct and honest, you allow the other person to move forward with dignity, even when the news is difficult.

From a management perspective, consistent one-on-one meetings are key. They're a structured opportunity to give and receive feedback. When someone does something well, I make it a point to say, "This was great; I really appreciated it." But when there's room for improvement, I'm equally direct: "I noticed in this email," or "I've observed this behavior, and here's what I'd like to see done differently."

It's important to address things as they come up rather than letting them pile up. And when they make improvements, I acknowledge that too: "You've really worked on this, and I appreciate the progress."

Beyond providing regular feedback, I've found it helpful to incorporate what I call "two-by-two feedback" into monthly or quarterly meetings, as suggested by the Management Center. Both the manager and the employee come prepared with feedback in four categories:

- Two pieces of affirming feedback for the other person (things they've done well)
- Two pieces of constructive feedback for the other person (areas for improvement)
- Two pieces of affirming feedback for themselves
- Two pieces of constructive feedback for themselves

This creates a balanced, collaborative discussion that is "both/and." For example, I might say to a team member, "I think you've done a great job on project management, *and* I'd like to see more attention to detail in your reports." They might respond, "Kevin, I appreciate how you send thoughtful, clear emails, *and* our check-ins often start late." It's now incumbent on both of us to accept the affirming feedback *and* work to address the adjusting feedback.

This consistent feedback loop makes it easier to normalize both praise and constructive criticism. When feedback is a regular part of the culture, it's not shocking or uncomfortable. It's just how things are done.

HOW TO HAVE TOUGH CONVERSATIONS

Tough conversations are never easy. So one of the things I do is to be intentional about choosing a space that allows the other person space to process, think, and come to terms with what's happening. Sometimes, I'll choose a coffee shop or restaurant close to the office but far enough away so no one from work can see what's going on.

This gives team members the option to head home afterward if they need time alone. That's part of recognizing humanity in these situations. When you tell someone that their financial situation is going to change by a certain date, it's an uncomfortable reality, no matter the timing or the location where the news is broken. Whether it's during the holidays or not, it's a big shift.

One of the fundamental expectations every employee has is the consistency of their pay. When that changes, you've altered the trajectory of their financial plans. You don't always know what they're dealing with. Maybe they're applying for a loan or looking for a new apartment, but your decision has impacted their life. That's why it's so important to approach these moments with empathy. You need to give them the space to grieve that loss, to process what it means for them. The tears or anger you see in that moment aren't always directed at you. Often, they're grieving the change and the loss of what once was.

If you're a leader preparing for an uncomfortable termination conversation, for instance, the first thing you need to understand is that less is more. Assuming you've already taken necessary performance improvement steps, this isn't the time for long explanations or attempts to soften the blow. You need to get straight to the point. When I've had these conversations, I've found that clarity and brevity are essential. I would walk into the room and say, "Today is going to be your last day." No buildup, no preamble. Just the truth.

As Ken Blanchard and Spencer John write in *The New One Minute Manager*, tell them "[W]hat they did wrong; tell them how you feel about it; and remind them they are better than that." In other words, "their performance is bad, but they are good."[48] Why approach it this way? Because the person needs to understand the gravity of the situation immediately.

You can explain the why briefly: "It's your last day because we've decided to move in a different direction," or whatever the specific reason might be. Then provide logistical details like when their pay will be deposited, when benefits will end, what the process is for clearing their office, and that they are no longer employed as of that day.

I know this may sound cold or harsh, but this is not the time for a "compliment sandwich," where you layer the bad news between positive comments. That approach only confuses the message. The individual needs to absorb the reality of the situation without false hope or ambiguity. Any attempt to soften the blow with excessive explanations or apologies can give the impression that there's room to reverse the decision, which only makes the process harder for both sides.

To put a finer point on it, Jesus got right to the point when discussing the pitfalls of judging others (Matthew 7:1–6); addressing

---

48 Ken Blanchard and Spencer Johnson, *The New One Minute Manager* (HarperCollins), loc. 842, Kindle.

religious leaders focused on religiosity instead of compassion for those in their care (Matthew 23:1–39); and even speaking with the disciples in his inner circle (Matthew 16:21–28). Pointed language is appropriate in the workplace and church settings. The apostle Paul said it this way in Romans 6:1–3: "So what do we do? Keep on sinning so God can keep on forgiving? I should hope not! If we've left the country where sin is sovereign, how can we still live in our old house there? Or didn't you realize we packed up and left there for good?"

Because leaders often fear the emotional reaction they might encounter during these conversations, they worry about finding the right words, striking the perfect tone, or managing the person's response. But here's the truth: *Nothing* you say will make it better. The news will hurt, and trying to sugarcoat it won't change that. So just deliver the message respectfully and let them begin to process it.

VOLUNTEER SETTINGS ARE MORE CHALLENGING

If you're a pastor, you know it's especially difficult to keep personnel matters from becoming personal. One of the reasons is that many of your personnel are volunteers. Because you aren't offering a paycheck, you're asking people to give their time and energy toward a goal, which can make feedback tricky.

In the church, everything is deeply personal. The relationships, the shared faith, and the sense of belonging make navigating challenges unique for pastors. One of the biggest hurdles is dealing with lay leaders or individuals who have stepped into power vacuums at moments when leadership was unclear or absent. They often hold tightly to those roles many years later, and shifting dynamics can feel like a threat to them.

Another challenge is that many people hold the church on a pedestal. Their life outside the church may be chaotic or lacking in control, and they long for comfort and stability. As a result, they tend to settle for "this is the way we've always done it." The church becomes the one place where they feel they can wield influence.

They cling to the familiar, even if it's not good for them, because it feels safe. That's why the phrase "We've never done it that way before" is often called the seven last words of a dying church. Pushing for change upsets this comfort, and people resist it, sometimes fiercely. In the Black church context, parishioners often protest with their feet or with their pocketbooks. That is, they take an extended leave of absence from service or choose to no longer support the church financially.

Likewise, church members often expect a sanctuary from conflict. People will say, "I deal with this at work. I didn't think I'd face it in church." But the truth is, there is no perfect church. Just as in any organization, the imperfections of its people shape the community. The church is a place where people bring their flaws, and those flaws inevitably show up.

If you're a pastor, you must recognize that pushback often stems from fear of the unknown. The challenge is balancing the need for change with the need to care for and guide people through their resistance. It's not easy, but it's necessary for the growth of the church—and the individuals within it.

Indeed, you cannot allow the fear of the impact of your decision on the number of attendees, choir members, ushers, or church or school participants to prevent you from making tough personnel choices. Inaction is also an action that can spell disaster in the future. By refusing to make the hard choices, you are perpetuating the status quo and making the matter harder for your successor to resolve later.

REMEMBER: PERSONNEL MATTERS SHOULD NOT BE PERSONAL

In summary, when it comes to handling personnel matters, there are a few key principles that I believe are essential for effective leadership.

First, approach every decision with humanity. Recognize that these decisions impact real people, their families, and their lives. While it's critical to treat people with dignity and respect, you must also remember that it's business, not personal. This distinction is essential. The decision isn't about your personal relationship with someone; it's about what's best for the ongoing function of the organization. That can be hard to navigate, but it's necessary.

Second, be prepared for the fallout. Sometimes, relationships you thought were strong may not survive these decisions. People may stop speaking to you or even distance themselves entirely. That's a risk you must be willing to take if you're going to lead effectively. Leadership often involves difficult choices, and those choices can have personal consequences. Inaction perpetuates the status quo.

Third, honor people for their contributions whenever possible. Celebrating someone's years of service doesn't mean they have to continue in their role. For example, we introduced the title of trustee emeritus at our church and recognized former trustees during our annual Trustee Day. They were no longer serving actively, but they were surprised and appreciative of the acknowledgment. You can create space for people to step back gracefully while still valuing their impact.

Fourth, remember that less is more. In tough conversations, clarity and brevity are crucial. Get to the heart of the matter quickly. When you overexplain or try to soften the blow with too many words, it can confuse the message and make it harder for the other person to process. Be concise and save the detailed reasoning for a later conversation if necessary.

Ultimately, the balance is in treating people with respect while remaining focused on the needs of the organization. It's not easy, but leading with humanity, clarity, and purpose will make these challenging moments a bit more manageable.

BULLETIN NOTES

KEY TAKEAWAYS:

- ☑ Effective leadership requires separating personal relationships from organizational decisions, ensuring clarity and fairness while addressing personnel matters.
- ☑ Tough conversations should prioritize brevity and clarity, delivering the message respectfully without confusing or softening the impact unnecessarily.
- ☑ Regular feedback and clear communication are essential to avoid surprises during performance reviews or terminations, fostering a culture of trust and growth.
- ☑ A balance of empathy and decisiveness helps leaders honor individuals' contributions while making decisions in the organization's best interest.

KEY QUESTIONS:

1. How can leaders cultivate a consistent feedback culture to ensure employees are never blindsided by performance evaluations or difficult decisions?
2. What strategies can be used to navigate personnel challenges in volunteer-driven or emotionally charged environments like churches?
3. How can leaders maintain personal integrity and organizational focus when their decisions risk damaging personal relationships?

PRINCIPLE 9

A Healthy Retreat Can Be a Sign of Strength

But those who wait for the Lord
Will gain new strength and renew their power;
They will lift up their wings like eagles
They will run and not become weary,
They will walk and not grow tired.

—ISAIAH 40:31 (AMPLIFIED BIBLE)

Retreat often feels like a dirty word. It's something we associate with weakness or failure, especially when we picture it in a military context. Baked into our minds is the attitude of the American general Douglas MacArthur: "We are not retreating. We are advancing in another direction."

But what if we viewed retreat in a different way? What if we saw it not as evidence we were giving up but a sign that we were stepping back, reassessing the situation, and focusing our energy where it matters most? In *Good to Great*, Jim Collins compares organizations that thrived to those that faltered. One example he shares is Kimberly-Clark, the maker of Kleenex. Early in its history, Kimberly-Clark was involved in both timber production and consumer products.

At a pivotal moment, the company's leadership boldly decided to sell its timberlands—a move that many at the time saw as a retreat from its core identity. It seemed risky and counterintuitive. However, the leadership recognized that its future wasn't in raw materials but in creating products like Kleenex.

Today, we don't think of Kimberly-Clark as a timber company. We think of Kleenex as so ubiquitous that it has become synonymous with tissues. That decision, which at the time may have felt like a failure to some, became the foundation for Kimberly-Clark's success. It was a purposeful retreat that allowed the company to focus its efforts and resources where they mattered most.

RETREAT SHOULD ALWAYS BE PURPOSEFUL

Now, let's apply that to Frederick Douglass, the charter school organization I joined in 2018. The organization had expanded from its original high school in Boston—a school that was one of the first fourteen charters in Massachusetts—to include additional campuses. By the time I arrived, this growth strategy had placed us in a precarious position. The decision to open a second school in Roxbury and another in New Bedford had stretched the organization thin.

The New Bedford campus was a challenge from day one. If you're not familiar with the region of New Bedford, it's a proud, insular community with a rich history. Once the leader in America's whaling industry, it's often called the Whaling City and is even mentioned in the second paragraph of *Moby Dick*. The city also has deep cultural roots, including a significant Cape Verdean population and a strong sense of identity that's distinct from Boston. New Bedford might as well be a world away in terms of how its residents view themselves in relation to Boston.

Frederick Douglass's leadership at the time thought they could replicate their Boston success in New Bedford, reasoning that both were "gateway cities" under Massachusetts charter law, communities with the greatest need to improve student academic outcomes. However, they underestimated the cultural differences and challenges of expanding into a community like New Bedford. The assumption was that if they built a school, families would enroll their children. But that's not how it played out. The "build it and they will come" mantra worked to Frederick Douglass's detriment.

From the start, enrollment at the New Bedford school was an issue. Families were skeptical, and the students who did enroll often came with significant academic and behavioral challenges. Many of these students had struggled in traditional schools and were looking for an alternative. But Frederick Douglass wasn't equipped to meet the level of support these students needed.

The school started under-enrolled and stayed that way. The space itself was inadequate for growth, and the organization lacked the resources to provide the level of academic and special needs support that students required. Meanwhile, the second Roxbury campus faced challenges of its own, trying to recruit students to a school within walking distance of the original location. Running three separate schools, each with insufficient enrollment, stretched the organization's finances and staff to a breaking point.

By the time I joined Frederick Douglass in 2018, the New Bedford school was on the brink. The organization had submitted an incomplete charter-renewal application to the state. I arrived on July 1, and by the end of the first month, I realized we were facing not just the risk of closure but also the potential loss of credibility as an organization.

The state's renewal process looks at a five-year track record, not the leadership or plans in place at the time of renewal. Despite any changes

I could make, we were being judged on the past five years—a period marked by underperformance and mismanagement. When the state granted a renewal, it came with probation, one step away from closure.

The commissioner of elementary and secondary education's letter acknowledged my arrival and the positive steps I was taking, but it didn't change the fact that the organization had failed to meet its commitments to students and families in New Bedford. That probation status made families uneasy. Many were hesitant to send their children to a school that might close. Enrollment dropped even further, highlighting that we were unable to turn things around.

At that point, I had to face the painful reality: the New Bedford school needed to close. But for me, this decision felt like a personal failure. I had relationships with families in New Bedford from my time as a pastor, and I felt I was letting them down.

But that's when one of my mentors helped shift my perspective. She reminded me of US Airways pilot Captain Chesley Sullenberger, affectionately known as Captain Sully, who landed a plane in the Hudson River in 2009.

"Kevin," she said, "no one remembers Sully for ditching the plane. They remember him for saving every life on board."

That analogy hit home, and I instantly knew how to reframe my situation. Closing the New Bedford school wasn't failure. It was a hard but necessary decision to prioritize the well-being of the students and the long-term health of the organization.

Surrendering the New Bedford charter allowed us to focus on the Boston schools, consolidating resources and creating a stronger foundation for the future. It also meant letting go of staff at the network office, which was painful but unavoidable. In hindsight, I see that retreat as a pivotal moment. It wasn't about giving up. It was about making space for something better.

Sometimes, the hardest thing we can do as leaders is acknowledge when something isn't working and make the decision to move in a different direction. Retreat, when done with purpose and integrity, isn't failure. It's strategy. It's the moment we step back, not to quit but to refocus, realign, and ultimately rise again.

RETREAT DOESN'T EQUAL FAILURE

That said, retreat does *not* come naturally to me. I'm the type of person who keeps going, pushing through challenges and tackling problems head on, no matter how difficult they seem. This relentless drive to keep moving forward is a core part of who I am, but it has also taught me the hardest lesson that not every battle is meant to be fought to the end.

While preparing a sermon series, I recently found myself reflecting on how the children of Israel captured Canaan. If you've read the Book of Joshua, for instance, you know their journey wasn't the smooth upward climb we often imagine. Their success wasn't linear. It was filled with highs and lows, setbacks and recoveries.

This perspective helped me reframe my view of my time at Frederick Douglass. When I arrived, the organization was in turmoil. I was the fourth leader in four years. Rapid expansion from one school to three had left the organization stretched thin and disjointed. Staff and community members alike were frustrated and confused. The creation of a network of schools, complete with a central office, added another layer of complexity.

Even during my first meeting with union representatives, it was clear how much misunderstanding there was. The union believed they were negotiating against a centralized network, but the reality was more complicated. I had to explain that I wasn't representing one unified entity but three separate charter schools, which would result in three separate union contracts. The staff's frustration was rooted in years of instability, missteps, and unmet expectations.

The unionization effort was not about me personally. I inherited the situation, but it reflected the significant challenges the organization faced. Leadership turnover had eroded trust. The decision to expand to New Bedford—a city the organization didn't fully understand—strained resources and morale. Staff were navigating a new network structure that they didn't completely grasp, which only heightened the tension. This environment of uncertainty had been growing for years, and I found myself in the midst of it.

At the time, it felt like a low point for Frederick Douglass and for me as a leader. But looking back, I see it differently. That period wasn't the end. It was the beginning of something new. It was an opportunity to reassess, confront the hard truths about what wasn't working, and lay the groundwork for a stronger future.

Retreat doesn't have to mean failure. Sometimes, it's the most strategic move you can make. It creates the space to realign with your mission, focus on what truly matters, and prepare for what's next. In the words of Norman Vincent Peale, "Masterly retreat is in itself a victory."

RETREAT HELPS US GAIN PERSPECTIVE

From a church perspective, the same drive to keep pushing through obstacles defines who I am today. Take my time at People's Institutional AME Church as an example. If the bishop hadn't moved me in 2019, I would still be there, working tirelessly to turn things around, hoping against hope, even if it meant driving myself into deeper debt.

To show you how intense my schedule was, back then I was teaching at the Ministerial Institute in New York. My class started at 7:30 a.m., so I'd leave the house at 3:30 a.m. to make it on time. Twice a month in the fall and winter, I made that drive to teach in the institute. But I loved it. Even in snowstorms, if there was a church meeting scheduled for 9:00 a.m., I'd leave as early as 4:00 a.m. to make sure I got there on time.

And sometimes when I arrived, the church steps and sidewalks hadn't been shoveled yet. Living in New England, I always had a shovel in my trunk, so I'd grab it and clear the snow myself. I'd often beat the members to the church and take care of it before they arrived. That's just who I am. If something needed to be done, I did it.

That's how I approach challenges. If I can't go around a problem, I'll find a way to go over it. If I can't go over it, I'll go under it. And if all else fails, I'll go straight through it. I'll push through the brick wall, and I'll inspire others to push with me because that's the kind of leader I am. I'll keep going until someone tells me to stop.

It reminds me of a story I once heard about a man who was asked by God to push a rock. Day after day, he pushed and pushed, but the rock never moved. Frustrated, he asked God, "Why did you ask me to push this rock if it wasn't going to move?"

And God replied, "I didn't ask you to move the rock. I asked you to push it. Look at how much stronger you've become. Your muscles have grown, and your perseverance has deepened." The man realized the purpose wasn't in moving the rock but in the transformation that came from pushing it.

That story resonates with me deeply. So much of my work feels like pushing a rock that doesn't move. At People's, I pushed as hard as I could, pouring myself into the mission, shoveling snow, driving through the night, and showing up for every challenge. When I left, I felt like I had let the church down because I hadn't "moved the rock."

But in hindsight, I see the strength I gained in the process. God didn't ask me to move the rock; he asked me to push it. And through that pushing, I grew stronger, wiser, and more prepared for the challenges ahead.

RETREAT HELPS YOU MOVE FORWARD

The COVID-19 pandemic was a time of retreat for many church leaders. It brought an unexpected and profound lesson for many of us in the ministry that the church is not the building. It's the people.

When the doors of our sanctuaries were forced shut, the question became how to stay connected with the congregation. For me, the answer began with what I was already doing. I kept reaching out and kept sending cards. That wasn't new, but it was something tangible that let people know they were seen and cared for.

From there, I added a monthly letter to every church member, updating them on the life of the church. For our seniors especially, this was a vital connection. Many of them felt isolated and missed the rhythm of Sunday gatherings. Others were eager to return to the sanctuary, even before we had denominational clearance to do so.

To bridge the gap, one of our associate ministers organized drive-by visits. We would stand outside a senior's home, socially distanced, waving, smiling, and delivering gift bags. It wasn't the same as meeting in person, but it was a way to remind them they were loved and not forgotten.

We needed to find creative ways to bring joy and engagement to the congregation. That's when I discovered Kahoot!, an online quiz platform. During the pandemic, it became our tool to gather virtually, have fun, and stay connected. I still have some Kahoot! games we played, such as What Is Advent? and Top Black Christmas Songs. After Sunday services, we played these games together as a congregation, maintaining the community spirit even while we were physically apart.

The pandemic taught us that church could thrive in new forms. Some online members were giving more financially than in-person members, and the reach of the church extended beyond physical walls. But it also taught us the importance of brevity and focus. People didn't want to sit through long, drawn-out Zoom services. You had to be concise and intentional, or they'd simply click over to another service.

In the time it used to take for one church service to end, people could attend two or three online. That's a reality we had to embrace. It was tough for many, but in time I've come to realize that a hard season of retreat laid the groundwork for many churches to move forward.

REFRAME YOUR RETREAT

If you're wrestling with the idea of stepping back or retreating, I would encourage you to think about how your legacy might take a different form than you expected.

For example, if you start a business and later decide to sell it or close it, that doesn't mean you failed. Selling to another company can extend your vision in ways you couldn't have achieved alone. Closing doesn't mean your idea wasn't good. Maybe the market wasn't ready, or the timing was off, but you still pushed the boundaries and made a difference. You positively impacted employees, customers, and your community. The legacy of your effort doesn't disappear just because the outcome isn't what you envisioned.

We often forget that life, like all things, has seasons. Even businesses or organizations have lifespans. When a beloved restaurant or shop closes, people mourn its loss, but that doesn't mean its existence wasn't meaningful. It played its role, served its purpose, and now the baton is passed to someone else to create something new. The same is true for any venture, church, or personal mission. Recognizing the natural life cycle of an endeavor doesn't diminish its value.

You must separate the success or failure of an organization from your personal identity. This is especially difficult for leaders, entrepreneurs, and pastors, who pour their hearts and souls into their work. It's easy to believe that the organization's fate reflects your worth, but that's simply not true. Yes, you might have been the visionary or the one driving the mission forward, but you are not the organization. Decisions like closing a division, retreating from a market, or stepping down from a leadership role are not reflections of failure. They are reflections of thoughtful leadership and prioritizing what's best for the organization, its stakeholders, and its people.

It's also important to keep perspective. Sometimes you need to step back and reflect to see the bigger picture. In the charter school world, we call this "getting on the balcony." It means stepping away from the daily grind and viewing the situation as if you were an outsider.

Taking time off, even briefly, allows you to separate your emotions from the work and reevaluate your role and decisions. When you're in the thick of it, it's easy to think brute force will solve every problem. But brute force is unsustainable. You might mortgage your house, work endless hours, and pour everything you have into the organization, but at what cost?

Sometimes the best thing you can do for yourself and your organization is retreat.

REMEMBER: A HEALTHY RETREAT CAN BE A SIGN OF STRENGTH

I think many leaders struggle with retreat because they buy into the notion that success is a straight line. As leaders, we create these expectations that every step forward will be an improvement over the last. We tell ourselves, "My next job will be better than this one," or "My next church will be bigger and more successful than the one I'm leading now."

We measure our worth by these metrics: earning more money, managing more people, or achieving higher levels of influence. However, success doesn't always follow that pattern. Sometimes, progress means taking a step back to ultimately move forward. Success isn't a straight line; it's a "best-fit curve," a term in mathematics that best represents the trend of data points. In other words, the best-fit curve considers the ups and downs, retreats, and triumphs.

I've experienced this firsthand. When I left Scholastic to join Denmark Vesey Charter Public Schools in 2012, I accepted a pay cut. On paper, it seemed like a step down, but it turned out to be one of the best decisions I've ever made. At Scholastic, there was no pathway for me to become the CFO or COO, let alone the CEO. The opportunities simply weren't available. By moving into the charter school sector, I created space to grow. I started as the associate director of revenue, was promoted to director of finance, and developed skills I never would have cultivated as a business manager in a billion-dollar corporation like Scholastic.

At the time, it felt like a risk. Taking less money and a lower title wasn't an easy decision. However, the reality is that, after taxes, the financial difference wasn't as significant as I had feared. Moreover, the experience I gained was invaluable. That move positioned me for the opportunities that arose later in my career, opportunities that would have been unattainable if I had remained in a more comfortable yet limiting role.

This is a principle we all understand in other areas of life. Think about driving in traffic. Sometimes, you must back up or take a detour to get where you're going. It's frustrating in the moment, but it's necessary. Yet, as leaders, we're often resistant to making those same choices in our professional lives. We fear that stepping back is a sign of failure when it can be the most strategic decision we make.

The key is redefining how we measure progress. Success is not always about earning more or leading bigger teams. Sometimes, it's about growth, about learning and preparing for what's next, even if it means letting go of certain titles or perks in the short term. Progress isn't a straight, upward trajectory. It's a series of peaks and valleys, and sometimes the best way forward is to take a step back, reassess, and choose a new path.

BULLETIN NOTES

KEY TAKEAWAYS:

- ☑ Retreat is a purposeful and strategic decision that allows individuals or organizations to reassess priorities and focus resources.
- ☑ It requires courage and perspective to acknowledge what isn't working and make hard decisions for long-term success.
- ☑ Success is nonlinear, often involving detours or setbacks that prepare for greater opportunities ahead.
- ☑ Retreat fosters growth, resilience, and alignment with one's mission, enabling stronger progress in the future.

KEY QUESTIONS:

1. How can leaders discern when it is time to retreat versus continuing to push forward in challenging situations?
2. What mindset shifts are necessary to reframe retreat as a strategic move rather than a failure?
3. How does viewing success as nonlinear impact the way individuals approach their personal and professional decisions?

PRINCIPLE 10

Be Intentionally Diverse

Diversity is the art of thinking independently together.

—MALCOLM FORBES

As I grew up in Ann Arbor, Michigan, my life was shaped by two powerful forces: the intellectual vibrancy of a college town and the close-knit, empowering community of Bethel.

Bethel AME Church, the largest Black church in the city, gave me a foundation in faith, leadership, and service that extended far beyond its walls. More than a place of worship, it was a hub of excellence where education, achievement, and community were celebrated and nurtured. These experiences at Bethel taught me the importance of being intentionally diverse—not just in how I saw myself but also in how I approached the world around me.

At Bethel, I was surrounded by educators, leaders, and professionals who poured their time and resources into shaping the next generation. Whether I was preparing for state tests or learning life skills like filling out a FAFSA (Free Application for Federal Student Aid) form, Bethel was a hub of empowerment for me. My parents, both educators, reinforced these lessons at home and in the community. My dad, for instance, modeled service by starting a lawn care business to support elderly church members, often bringing me along to teach me the value of hard work and caring for others. This sense of responsibility became a core part of who I am.

Those lessons carried with me into the Ann Arbor Public Schools, a district shaped by the diversity of the University of Michigan's community of students, professors, and researchers. My classmates often came from academic or international backgrounds, and I found myself sitting beside the children of UM professors and graduate students. Yet, even in a relatively progressive city, racism and microaggressions cropped up in the classroom. My parents had a front-row seat to these challenges. My mother taught elementary school in the district for more than three decades, and my father worked as a motor coach operator at the university for just as long. Their example, combined with Bethel's lessons, prepared me to face those realities head on.

Bethel instilled in me a pride in my Blackness and equipped me with the tools to navigate spaces where I might be the only person of color. I learned to code switch, a skill that proved invaluable in a predominantly white school district, especially within high-level academic settings like AP classes and the National Honor Society. Rather than fading into the background, I felt ready to excel and be recognized. That confidence propelled me into leadership roles, such as vice president of the student council in fourth grade, president of the Black student union in eighth grade, class president, and Midwest regional parliamentarian for Jack and Jill of America, Inc., in my senior year. These experiences taught me how to thrive in environments where diversity wasn't a given but rather something to be actively cultivated.

One of my most defining moments came at age thirteen when I spoke during a Rev. Dr. Martin Luther King Jr. celebration at Bethel. Standing before the congregation and sharing Dr. King's legacy awakened me to the power of words and my responsibility to use my voice for good. That experience, coupled with Bethel's constant encouragement, gave me confidence that carried over into every aspect of my life. Moments like these weren't just lessons in public speaking; they were lessons in leadership and contribution.

When I arrived at Tuskegee University—one of the "Black Ivies"—I found myself among driven Black students whose achievements rivaled my own. That environment reinforced what Bethel had taught me: I belonged among those who expected excellence of themselves and others. My upbringing gave me a unique perspective that helped me embrace diverse viewpoints, even in unexpected places.

Not all my professors at Tuskegee were Black, and while some classmates distrusted these white professors, my experiences in Ann Arbor had shaped me to be open minded. I believed each person could bring value to the table, a lesson that served me well in building connections across differences in race, gender, religion, sexual orientation, and political views.

It was at Tuskegee that I first heard Zora Neale Hurston's quote "All my skin folk ain't my kinfolk." That sentiment resonated deeply, teaching me that allyship[49] can come in many forms. Just as not everyone who looks like me shares my values, not everyone who looks different from me is an adversary. Growing up at Bethel, navigating Ann Arbor, and thriving at Tuskegee taught me to seek common ground and value the power of intentionally building diverse alliances.

These lessons didn't stay confined to the classroom or church. They shaped my approach to leadership and ministry. Whether I was dining with the president of Ford Motor Company at a scholarship luncheon or leading student organizations, I relied on the foundation Bethel had given me.

---

49 A social justice practice that involves supporting and advocating for marginalized groups.

Bethel taught me that faith and education were deeply intertwined, and its emphasis on excellence, service, and resilience prepared me to walk confidently into any room. It was the foundation that shaped who I am today. It taught me that excellence is the norm, allyship is powerful, and faith is most impactful when it is lived out in service to others. These lessons continue to guide me in every space I enter.

Whether it's creating opportunities for youth, recognizing academic milestones, or fostering a sense of belonging, I strive to replicate the environment of encouragement and growth that Bethel provided for me.

DEI IS A MARATHON

The work of diversity, equity, and inclusion (DEI) is a marathon more than it is a sprint. For many, the murder of George Floyd was a catalyst. The world watched in 2020 as a Black Minnesota man called out for his mother while a police officer knelt on his neck for nearly nine minutes, tragically ending his life.

The horror of that moment sparked outrage, protests, and a rush to address systemic racism. For some, it was a wake-up call. But for others—especially those of us who live with the daily realities of racial inequity—it was simply another milestone on a much longer journey. For leaders like me, DEI work didn't begin with George Floyd. It began long before, shaped by countless experiences of microaggressions, racial profiling, and moments where I was underestimated because of the color of my skin.

The true challenge lies in maintaining momentum after the headlines fade and the cameras move on. It's easy to care when the world is watching, but where is the outrage when day-to-day inequities persist? Where is the righteous indignation when I enter a store and am followed by security, or when I'm told I lack "sector-specific experience" despite leading the largest climate tech incubator in North America?

This is the test of commitment. For many organizations, their DEI focus was only "George Floyd deep." The initial outrage led to training sessions, committees, and glossy website updates about their commitment to inclusion. But as soon as the news cycle moved on or public attention waned, so did their commitment. DEI became an expendable line item, easily cut when it was no longer convenient.

This performative approach misses the entire point. True DEI work isn't about responding to headlines. It's about addressing the structural inequities that persist long after the cameras are gone. I like Beverly Tatum's concept of the "moving walkway" in her book *Why Are All the Black Kids Sitting Together in the Cafeteria?* She writes,

> I sometimes visualize the ongoing cycle of racism as a moving walkway at the airport. Active racist behavior is equivalent to walking fast on the conveyor belt. The person engaged in active racist behavior has identified with the ideology of White supremacy and is moving with it. Passive racist behavior is equivalent to standing still on the walkway. No overt effort is being made, but the conveyor belt moves the bystanders along to the same destination as those who are actively walking. Some of the bystanders may feel the motion of the conveyor belt, see the active racists ahead of them, and choose to turn around, unwilling to go to the same destination as the White supremacists. But unless they are walking actively in the opposite direction at a speed faster than the conveyor belt—unless they are actively antiracist—they will find themselves carried along with the others.[50]

50 Beverly Daniel Tatum, *Why Are All the Black Kids Sitting Together in the Cafeteria?: And Other Conversations about Race* (New York: Basic Books, n.d.), 116.

Tatum's point is clear: To be antiracist, you must actively turn and walk against that momentum. It's exhausting, relentless work. The truth is real DEI work isn't optional or temporary. It's not something you add to a list of priorities only to cut when times get tough. It's a lens through which every decision must be made.

Hiring practices, vendor selection, promotions, recruitment—all of it must be viewed through the lens of diversity, equity, and inclusion. This isn't just an add-on or a box to check. It's about reshaping the systems that perpetuate inequity and creating organizations that reflect the values they claim to hold.

We've seen this struggle before. After Reconstruction, the progress of freed Black Americans was met with the backlash of Jim Crow. The election of President Obama was hailed by some as the beginning of a post-racial America, yet it was followed by a wave of racial resentment and the rise of Trumpism. History repeats itself when we fail to address the underlying issues. The "vestiges of slavery," as cited in *Brown v. Board of Education*, still shape our society today. But if we whitewash history to spare certain groups discomfort, we undermine the truth and lose the opportunity to create meaningful change.

As a leader of color, I've watched how uncomfortable these conversations make people. I've also seen how organizations backpedal when the work becomes challenging. But the truth remains: This isn't about short-term fixes or symbolic gestures. It's about long-term, sustained effort. If DEI isn't embedded into the DNA of an organization, it will always be at risk of being deprioritized. It cannot be an afterthought, a third or fourth bullet point on a strategic plan. It has to be the lens through which every action and decision is evaluated.

The work of DEI is challenging. It requires confronting uncomfortable truths, acknowledging privilege, and actively opposing systems of oppression. It is not a one-time event or a reaction to a singular tragedy. It is a lifelong commitment to justice, equity, and the belief that everyone deserves to be seen, valued, and treated with dignity.

As Austin Channing Brown notes, "A great many people believe that reconciliation boils down to dialogue: a conference on race, a lecture, a moving sermon about the diversity we'll see in heaven. But dialogue is productive toward reconciliation only when it leads to action—when it inverts power and pursues justice for those who are most marginalized."[51] For those who are truly committed, the journey continues long after the headlines fade. It's not about a sprint to the next crisis. It's about running the marathon, knowing the work is far from over.

DIVERSITY COMES IN MANY FORMS

From a church perspective, many churches have struggled with diminished women's voices. In almost any congregation, women make up the majority in the pews, yet men still occupy most of the leadership roles.

In my denomination, the African Methodist Episcopal (AME) Church, there's a worldwide organization called AME/Women in Ministry. It's designed to recognize and support women in ministry as an integral part of the AME Church; raise awareness of women's issues within the denomination; address sexism in the AME Church; and work to expand leadership opportunities for women in ministry globally, among other initiatives.

The AME Church began in 1787 and was incorporated in 1816, yet it wasn't until the year 2000 that we elected and consecrated our first female bishop. Her name is Bishop Vashti Murphy McKenzie, and she's an exceptional leader. Consider that timeline: nearly two

---

51 Austin Channing Brown, *I'm Still Here: Black Dignity in a World Made for Whiteness* (New York: Crown Publishing Group, 2018), 169.

centuries passed before a woman had a seat on the bench of bishops. Only in 2016 did we finally posthumously ordain Jarena Lee, acknowledging that she should have been ordained in the 1830s when she was alive. Furthermore, it would take more than two decades after Bishop McKenzie's ascent for a female to be elected first on the ballot when Bishop Erika D. Crawford did so in 2024.

Having more women on the bench, or the Council of Bishops, has brought women's experiences front and center in the church. This has helped shape policies and conversations in a denomination that, despite having mostly female congregants, has operated under male-driven traditions for a very long time. Ultimately, the more diverse voices there are at the table, the better churches can address those needs.

You see similar tensions around race too. Some might question whether a church that emphasizes its historical roots as an "African Methodist Episcopal" body is unwelcoming to others. Yet part of being intentionally diverse means acknowledging our origins: the AME Church was founded in Philadelphia in 1787 as a protest movement when Black worshipers were denied the right to pray at the same altar as white congregants. Our founder, Bishop Richard Allen, was one of the unsung Founding Fathers of the United States. He was, for instance, the first African American to eulogize President George Washington in 1799. Holding on to that, history doesn't exclude anyone; it simply keeps us rooted in our values of freedom and justice.

We see the need for diversity in other areas as well. Take government, for example. Policies like equal pay or parental leave wouldn't be on the table if women hadn't been elected to Congress and pushed for them. The same principle applies to the church. If the leadership table includes only men, or only older folks, or people from certain backgrounds, the perspectives and needs of other groups will be overlooked. True diversity, whether in a church or any organization, introduces new ideas, challenges groupthink, and ensures that everyone's voice is heard.

That means inviting younger members, embracing people across the spectrum of gender identities, and valuing racial and ethnic differences. Diversity in the church is both a reflection of the kingdom of God and a practical necessity for meeting the real, everyday needs of the people we're called to serve.

BE INTENTIONALLY DIVERSE

Being intentionally diverse means creating a culture where diversity isn't a box to check or a marketing veneer. It's an essential ingredient in how we think, operate, and grow. It recognizes that diverse teams bring sharper perspectives, richer ideas, and more innovative solutions.

In Patrick Lencioni's *The Five Dysfunctions of a Team*, he describes the importance of mining for conflict. He writes, "Mining Members of teams that tend to avoid conflict must occasionally assume the role of a 'miner of conflict'—someone who extracts buried disagreements within the team and sheds the light of day on them. They must have the courage and confidence to call out sensitive issues and force team members to work through them."[52]

If everyone in a room looks alike, thinks alike, and has similar life experiences, the group is far more likely to ignore or dismiss key insights. True diversity—of race, gender, sexual orientation, background, and thought—ensures you have people willing to offer that different perspective.

Yet too often, leaders of color face tokenism or a phenomenon called the glass cliff, where they're placed in positions with little chance

52 Patrick M. Lencioni, *The Five Dysfunctions of a Team: A Leadership Fable*, 20th Anniversary ed. (J-B Lencioni Series Book 43) (Hoboken, NJ: Wiley, 2024), 204–5.

of success. If they fail, organizations justify not seeking out diverse leadership again: "We tried that once, and it didn't work."

This mindset misses the point entirely. Being intentionally diverse means giving leaders of color the same support, resources, and runway to grow that others receive. It also means recognizing that the aim isn't to exclude anyone but to intentionally include those who've historically been overlooked.

REMEMBER: BE INTENTIONALLY DIVERSE

As leaders, whether we are pastors or CEOs, we often assume diversity will happen on its own. We believe it can develop naturally, without specific goals or focused steps. In practice, however, that rarely works. When you look around the leadership table and see people who share the same background, education, or worldview, that uniformity is not accidental. It reflects unconscious biases, the inclination to hire or promote individuals who remind us of ourselves.

Real diversity of thought reveals new possibilities and disrupts groupthink. When we include voices with varied experiences, cultures, and perspectives, we discover fresh solutions. This seldom occurs by chance when we rely on the same networks we have always used. Sometimes we must be intentional and accept discomfort to move beyond old habits.

This approach demands self-awareness about unconscious bias, our privilege, and the intrinsic nature of patriarchy. Even well-intentioned leaders tend to hire or collaborate with people who mirror their outlooks. While this may feel safe, it maintains the status quo. By committing to diversity, we begin to see our blind spots. Valuing many perspectives is not a single training or a box to check; it is a daily lens for decisions.

In the words of Jemar Tisby, "Diversity in leadership is an absolute must-have if an organization desires diversity."[53] Building a leadership team that does not match us in every way can feel unsettling at first, yet that tension often leads to growth. In churches and corporate settings, leaders improve when they stretch beyond their comfort zone. That shift moves us away from an echo chamber and gives fresh ideas space to take root. The result is stronger decisions and a culture where every voice can be heard, not just the loudest or the most familiar.

BULLETIN NOTES

KEY TAKEAWAYS:

- ☑ Being intentionally diverse means actively seeking and fostering a culture where diverse perspectives, experiences, and voices are valued and included in decision-making.
- ☑ True diversity goes beyond race and gender to include differences in thought, background, and experience, which leads to richer ideas and innovative solutions.
- ☑ Diversity requires intentional leadership and cannot be left to chance, as unconscious biases often perpetuate homogeneity in teams and organizations.
- ☑ Long-term diversity, equity, and inclusion efforts demand continuous commitment and systemic change rather than temporary, reactionary measures.

53 Jemar Tisby, *How to Fight Racism: Courageous Christianity and the Journey toward Racial Justice* (Grand Rapids, MI: Zondervan, 2021), 92.

KEY QUESTIONS:

1. How can leaders identify and address unconscious biases that hinder diversity in their teams or organizations?
2. What steps can organizations take to ensure diversity efforts are sustained and not just temporary reactions to societal events?
3. In what ways can leaders create opportunities for marginalized voices to be genuinely heard and valued within their communities or workplaces?

PRINCIPLE 11

Stand Firm in the Face of Opposition

Don't be afraid of a little opposition. Remember that the 'Kite' of success generally rises AGAINST the wind of Adversity, not with it.[54]

—NAPOLEON HILL

Leadership is not just about progress. It is about standing firm in the face of opposition and navigating the tension that inevitably comes with meaningful change. If you have ever faced pushback against a decision rooted in your principles, whether at work, in your community, or within your own family, you know the weight of leadership under pressure.

Resistance is not just a clash of ideas; it often reflects a deeper discomfort with letting go of what feels secure. As German philosopher Arthur Schopenhauer wrote, "All truth passes through three stages. First, it is ridiculed. Second, it is violently opposed. Third, it is accepted as being self-evident."[55] People cling to the familiar, even

54 Napoleon Hill, *The Law of Success: The Master Wealth-Builder's Complete and Original Lesson Plan for Achieving Your Dreams* (New York: Penguin, 2008), 27.

55 Arthur Schopenhauer, *101 Facts of Life* (Publishdrive, 2016), 4.

when it holds them back, because stepping into the unknown can feel terrifying.

As a leader, your greatest challenge is not just to offer solutions but to remain unwavering as you guide others through uncertainty. True leadership emerges not from avoiding conflict but from standing firm with clarity, grace, and resilience, even when the path is fraught with challenges.

History is full of examples of leaders who stood firm in the face of fierce opposition: abolitionists fighting for freedom, suffragists advocating for equality, and civil rights leaders marching for justice. These moments of progress were rarely welcomed with open arms. They were hard won through courage, endurance, and the resolve to push forward despite resistance. The same holds true in your own leadership journey.

Opposition is not always a sign of failure; it is often proof that the work you are doing matters, and that real change is underway.

SOMETIMES IT FEELS LIKE EVERYONE IS AGAINST YOU

Going back to my time at Frederick Douglass, I knew the choice to surrender the New Bedford charter was right, yet nothing prepared me for the wave of opposition that followed. Once we confirmed we had to close the school at the end of the year, Massachusetts charter law required us to hold a public meeting within a strict time frame.

That meeting took place on a Monday evening in December 2019, in a room that served as both a cafeteria and a gathering space. People filled every seat, and those who couldn't find a place to sit stood around the edges. At the front, I stood with our board chair, while several board members and a representative from the state's charter authorizer sat nearby.

From the moment I began explaining why we were surrendering the charter, anger rippled through the crowd. Parents accused me of lying, others said we had broken promises, and voices kept rising. A tenth-grade student climbed onto a cafeteria table, screaming that nobody was listening to her. Someone even called the police, and I remember standing near an officer, watching this outpouring of frustration, knowing I had to maintain composure.

Much of their anger was directed at me, even though I had only joined the organization a year prior. I hadn't made the original promise to these families, but I had become the face they associated with the school. It was hard to see them so upset, knowing I couldn't provide the outcome they desired. Some insisted that I was choosing to close the school without any consideration for student needs. In actuality, we had lost the ability to serve our students adequately. Special education services required specific funding and staff that we no longer had. We owed it to these young people to acknowledge that we couldn't meet their needs.

In parallel, we faced a different challenge in Boston. We had two Frederick Douglass charters located on two campuses, each with lower enrollment than projected. Our solution, never attempted in Massachusetts charter history, was colocation. We decided to put ninth and tenth graders from both charters in one building and eleventh and twelfth graders from both charters in another, halfway across the neighborhood. On paper, this plan saved money and ensured full classrooms. But parents felt blindsided. They had enrolled their children at one campus for its location, and now we were asking them to switch midyear.

We organized another public meeting. This time, the space was bigger, and all board members were present, but it was equally contentious. Parents accused me of endangering their children by sending them to a more commercial area rather than a residential neighborhood. One father compared the plan to placing rival gangs together in the "yard," a reference to the gathering place of inmates in prisons.

I remember thinking how strange it was to hear him describe teenagers—his child among them—like hardened criminals. The meeting felt like a never-ending surge of complaints. Many insisted they would never agree to send their children across town. Yet by the end of the school year, most students stayed, and I learned a series of valuable lessons in the aftermath.

IMPORTANT LESSONS I LEARNED

These experiences taught me that making the right choice often provokes fierce resistance. Nobody likes to see a school close or endure a major restructuring, and I had to accept that I would be the target of much of that frustration. Some critics wanted me fired immediately, and newspapers questioned my leadership. Yet I had to stand firm because the numbers indicated we couldn't survive otherwise. We did what was necessary, and although the public meetings unsettled me, they strengthened my resolve.

I also grew in my ability to handle conflict and was reminded that anger is not the answer. As Gordon MacDonald writes, "A driven person often possesses a volcanic force of anger, which can erupt anytime he senses opposition or disloyalty."[56] I sensed this tension when I was challenged, but through not giving in, I grew as a person.

Additionally, I learned how vital it is to celebrate small victories. When parents threatened to leave en masse but most students remained, that *was significant.* When Boston enrollment proved steadier than we expected, that was important too. Leadership isn't

---

56 Gordon MacDonald, *Ordering Your Private World* (Nashville: Thomas Nelson, 2007), 38.

about constant triumphs. It's about striving for a larger goal, even when victories are rare, and setbacks prevail. There will be instances of tension, anger, and heartbreak before that moment of relief comes.

Ultimately, I realized that you only need a core group committed to moving forward. I had a supportive board, a strong executive team, and student-focused principals who believed we were making the best decision given the circumstances. That small circle provided me the courage to see things through. Not every parent, student, or community member supported the change, but enough did so that we could follow the plan.

Closing the New Bedford school and colocating the Boston campuses felt like two battles happening at once, each with its own intensity. Both taught me what real leadership under pressure requires: honesty about what you can and cannot deliver, endurance when criticism grows loud, and an unwavering focus on the long-term health of the mission—even if it means enduring anger and heartbreak in the process.

OPPOSITION CAN BE A GOOD SIGN

I wouldn't say I thrive on opposition, but I do believe it often indicates progress. A good idea doesn't always inspire everyone to jump on board right away. When people push back, they might be mourning the loss of what once felt secure. They're stepping out of their comfort zone, where they relied on themselves rather than on faith or a less certain path. That kind of leap can be unsettling. If we acknowledge that discomfort is part of growth, we can see resistance as evidence that real change is happening.

I often reflect on the story of the butterfly struggling to escape its cocoon. Noticing this struggle, a young boy attempted to help by cutting the cocoon with scissors, hoping to make the butterfly's emergence easier. Unfortunately, the result was not what the boy expected. The butterfly did emerge, but its wings never fully developed, preventing it from flying. It turns out that the friction of pushing through the cocoon is essential for maturing the wings. Without that struggle, the butterfly cannot take flight. Thus, the process of refining—whether through fire for clay or tension for a cocoon—cannot be skipped.

Much like the civil rights movement, meaningful change is never accomplished in a single day or through a single action. It is the result of consistent, tireless effort over time, often in the face of great resistance and adversity. While the iconic marches, speeches, and landmark victories of the civil rights movement are remembered and celebrated, those moments were the culmination of countless hours of unrecognized work—grassroots organizing, quiet strategy sessions, and small but vital acts of courage.

The spotlight may have illuminated the most dramatic moments, but real progress was made behind the scenes, away from the cameras, in the hearts and minds of those committed to justice. This serves as a powerful reminder that while recognition and momentum can provide inspiration, true change requires a relentless commitment to the mission long after the headlines fade.

In navigating these ongoing challenges, I find energy and purpose by focusing on the long-term vision rather than the immediate obstacles. It is not always easy to move forward when the path is uncertain or when progress seems painfully slow, but leadership demands the ability to see the light at the end of the tunnel, even if that light is faint and far away. Encouraging others to hold on to hope in such moments is not just an act of motivation; it is an act of leadership.

By reframing challenges as opportunities for growth and perseverance, I aim to help others see that every step, no matter how small, brings us closer to meaningful change. As President John F. Kennedy noted, "There will always be dissident voices heard in the land, expressing opposition without alternatives, finding fault but never favor, perceiving gloom on every side and seeking influence without responsibility."[57] But even in the most difficult times, I remind myself and those around me that persistence, faith, and unwavering commitment are what transform dreams into reality.

DISTINGUISH BETWEEN CRITICISM AND OPPOSITION

Some opposition, if it's in the form of constructive criticism, can be a helpful tool in shaping a plan. Stephen Covey reinforced this by writing, "We develop our character muscles by overcoming challenges and obstacles."[58] When someone points out a flaw or draws attention to a blind spot I hadn't seen before, that critique helps me refine my thinking.

However, opposition out of bad intent is very different. It's not about refining the plan; it's about stopping it cold. Saboteurs will say things like "This is the worst idea ever," or "I'll do everything I can to thwart this." They're not looking to negotiate or improve; they simply want to prevent the idea from moving forward.

---

57 John F. Kennedy, "Undelivered Speech to the Dallas Citizens Council, Intended for Delivery on 22 November 1963, Trade Mart, Dallas, Texas," JFK Library, https://www.jfklibrary.org/asset-viewer/archives/jfkpof-048-022#?image_identifier=JFKPOF-048-022-p0001.

58 Stephen R. Covey, A. Roger Merrill, and Rebecca R. Merrill, *First Things First Every Day: Daily Reflections—Because Where You're Headed Is More Important Than How Fast You Get There* (New York: Simon and Schuster, 1997), 115.

Some folks will form coalitions to shoot down anything new, while others, even if they have doubts, will say, "OK, let's see where this leads. Maybe if we adjust a few details, we can make it work." Those are the people you can collaborate with, even if you don't always see eye to eye. It ties back to the principle of being able to disagree in private, offer your honest input, and then commit to the final decision and carry it forward together.

Within every church and organization, there's usually a small group of people who consistently resist any form of change. Dr. Dolly Chugh, a professor at New York University, taught a workshop I attended. She broke it down like this: If you take any group of people, about 20 percent will support you right away, another 20 percent will oppose you no matter what, and the remaining 60 percent can be persuaded one way or another. Those who oppose you, sometimes simply out of habit, can still influence that middle 60 percent. So it becomes crucial to reach the persuadable majority and to understand the objections of the opposition—without dismissing them as ignorant or irrelevant. That doesn't mean you'll always bring them on board, but you avoid handing them a rallying cry.

In the end, if there's a determined 20 percent who will never agree, your focus shifts to convincing that middle group. You rely on the initial supporters to energize you for that work. It's never about beating up on the critics. It's about being clear, staying open to valid concerns, and always remembering there are plenty of people who haven't made up their minds yet. That's where the real potential for progress lies.

"STAND FIRM" IS A BIBLICAL COMMAND

The Bible consistently encourages believers to stand firm in their faith and trust in God. In 1 Corinthians 16:13, we are urged to "stand firm in the faith; be courageous; be strong." Similarly, Philippians 1:27 calls us to "stand firm in the one Spirit, striving together as one for the faith of the gospel," while Galatians 5:1 reminds us to stand firm in the freedom Christ provides. Ephesians 6:13–14 emphasizes the importance of putting on the full armor of God to "stand your ground" and resist evil, and 2 Thessalonians 2:15 encourages holding fast to the teachings passed on to us.

Moses, in Exodus 14:13, instructs the Israelites to "stand firm and you will see the deliverance the Lord will bring you today." In the New Testament, 1 Peter 5:9 tells believers to resist the devil and stand firm in faith, while Isaiah 7:9 warns that "if you do not stand firm in your faith, you will not stand at all." James 5:8 also urges patience and steadfastness as we anticipate the Lord's coming.

The founder of Methodism, John Wesley, put it this way: "Unless God has raised you up for this very thing, you will be worn out by the opposition of men and devils. But if God be for you, who can be against you? Are all of them together stronger than God? O be not weary of well doing!"[59]

Like Wesley, I've discovered that sometimes the toughest opposition comes from within the church. Case in point, my wife and I had just bought our New England home in February 2021 when, in June, I was assigned to pastor at Israel in Albany, two hours away. The congregation had worked hard to renovate their parsonage, raising almost $100,000 on their own. By church rules, I had the right to

---

59 John Wesley, *John Wesley* (Oxford: Oxford University Press, 1980), 86.

move into the parsonage. But since my family was already settled, I chose to stay in our new house.

That decision sparked immediate tension. Some members were upset, saying, "If I had known you weren't going to live here, I wouldn't have put in such high-end finishes in the parsonage." Others shrugged it off, saying it was my choice and an opportunity to build generational wealth. I tried to remind them that their renovation fundraising was ultimately for the good of the church, not for me personally. If the investment was truly dedicated to God's work, it shouldn't matter who lived in the building.

Then came the next challenge: What if we rented the parsonage? Finances were tight, and renting could provide stable income. Yet many felt the pastor's home was sacred property and should never be used that way. We debated this in long meetings, took votes, and endured heated discussions before finally agreeing to rent it out.

But once a tenant moved in, we had to settle a new question: Where should the rental income go? The trustees believed they should keep it all because they'd be responsible for maintaining church property. I argued that a share of that money ought to go to the wider church budget. Again, it took rounds of debate until we worked out a profit-sharing arrangement that helped both sides.

Meanwhile, I encouraged the church's food ministry to become more self-sufficient instead of relying solely on tithes and offerings. Some members opposed this idea because it challenged the traditional way of doing things. However, shortly after we approved the plan—by a narrow margin—an organization stepped in and donated $7,000 worth of food, which was more than half our annual budget. Nobody had anticipated that, and it reminded me that if we're open to trying something new, blessings can come in unexpected ways.

Moments like these continued to unfold. A few individuals who disagreed with my proposals withheld their donations or refused to maintain the leadership roles they had held for years. During Advent, one member decided she would no longer decorate the church at all, hoping that this would reflect poorly on me. Instead of scrambling to resolve the decorating crisis, I chose to let it go. Advent, after all, is about the birth of Jesus, not merely wreaths and poinsettias, garlands and bows. We still enjoyed a joyful Christmas celebration, and the lack of decorations didn't prevent us from worshipping.

What I've learned is that strong opposition often emerges at each stage of real change. Some folks become intimidated when old habits or power structures shift, and they'll do anything they can to stall progress. Others feel attached to tradition and find it painful to do anything differently. Through it all, I've tried to stay consistent: give people space to voice their concerns, follow the best path for the church, and trust that God can bring about outcomes none of us foresee.

This story is proof that, despite the bumps and battles, forward motion is possible—and sometimes, doors open that you never even knew existed.

REMEMBER: STAND FIRM IN THE FACE OF OPPOSITION

While opposition is inevitable, your response to it can go in one of two directions. You can let it make you a stronger person, or you can allow the hardships you face to turn you into a cynic. It's undeniably hard to keep from growing cynical, especially as you get older, and the weight of persistent struggles begins to feel heavier.

Whether it's in leadership, in ministry, or simply in trying to make a difference, it can feel like the effort is swallowed up by resistance and inertia. But when those thoughts creep in, I try to reframe my perspective and draw from history, faith, and the collective wisdom of others. I do this because I don't want to become a cynical person.

Leadership author Carey Nieuwhof writes, "My theory goes like this: As you grow older, you become more of who you already are. Just like your body stiffens a bit, your personality becomes less flexible. It's like there's this war inside you that's battling for hope—and cynicism will win, or it will lose. But you won't just be a little cynical or a little hopeful. The die is cast, and the concrete hardens."[60]

We often romanticize the civil rights movement as a series of grand, sweeping victories: the Montgomery Bus Boycott, the March on Washington for Jobs and Freedom, the Selma to Montgomery March, the Voting Rights Acts. These iconic moments get all the attention, but they were the culmination of countless small, local efforts—coalitions, conversations, and community meetings that didn't make headlines. The people involved in those small acts of persistence didn't know if they would ever see the fruits of their labor. Yet, they believed that their work was part of something greater, a cumulative effort that would one day make a difference.

That's what keeps me going. Even when I can't see the waterfall ahead, I must trust that the drops of water we're contributing will one day join the torrent. It's the belief that the work matters, even if the results aren't immediate or visible in my lifetime. Cynicism creeps in when we lose sight of that bigger picture, when we start believing that our small contributions don't add up. But history shows us otherwise. The change we see today is the result of people who didn't give up, even when the path seemed insurmountable.

---

60 Carey Nieuwhof, *Didn't See It Coming: Overcoming the Seven Greatest Challenges That No One Expects and Everyone Experiences* (New York: Crown Publishing Group, 2018), 21.

I also remind myself that this isn't just about me. I might feel disheartened, but what happens if I give up? If I step away from leadership or stop contributing to the causes I care about, who will take my place? Who will fix what's broken? There's a responsibility that comes with being called to do this work, and I remind myself that quitting isn't just a personal decision—it has consequences for others.

That's not to say it's easy. There are days when I feel like I'm pushing a boulder uphill, only to have it roll back down. In those moments, I lean on my community. I reach out to colleagues and friends who understand the struggle. We share our frustrations, but more importantly, we encourage one another to keep going. There's a strength in knowing you're not alone, that others are walking the same path and are willing to help carry the load.

Faith also plays a huge role in fighting cynicism. When I reflect on Dr. Maya Angelou's words—that we are "the hope and the dream of the slave"—I feel both humbled and inspired. No matter how bad things may seem, we are living in a reality that someone else dreamed of and prayed earnestly for. We're proof that progress is possible, even if it's imperfect. That perspective reminds me that giving up isn't an option. The work we do today is the foundation for someone else's tomorrow.

Ultimately, staying open to others and resisting the pull of cynicism is about choosing hope, even when it feels naive or futile. It's about believing that your small actions matter and that they're part of a larger story that's still unfolding. The world might not change overnight, and victories might not come as often as we'd like, but they do come.

And when they do, they're a testament to the perseverance of those who refused to give up, even when it would've been easier to retreat into cynicism. That's the ultimate motivator for me: the belief that what we do, no matter how small, is part of something far greater than ourselves. This gives me the strength to stand firm.

BULLETIN NOTES

KEY TAKEAWAYS:

☑ Standing firm in the face of opposition is not just a test of leadership but often a sign that meaningful change is underway.

☑ Resistance frequently stems from discomfort with leaving the familiar, requiring leaders to guide others through uncertainty with clarity and resilience.

☑ Small, consistent efforts behind the scenes are often more impactful than public recognition, proving that true progress requires persistence and commitment.

☑ Opposition is not always destructive; it can be an opportunity for refining ideas, strengthening resolve, and building a long-term vision.

KEY QUESTIONS:

1. How can you differentiate between constructive criticism and opposition aimed solely at preventing progress?
2. When faced with resistance, what strategies can you use to maintain composure and stay committed to your long-term vision?
3. How do you inspire others to see the potential for growth and change when the path forward appears uncertain or difficult?

PRINCIPLE 12

Swing for the Fences

I've always swung the same way. The difference is when I swing and miss, people say, "He's swinging for the fences." But when I swing and make contact people say, "That's a nice swing." But there's no difference, it's the same swing.

—SAMMY SOSA

While great leaders are strategic and thoughtful, they are also incredibly ambitious. They think big, dream big, and act boldly. In baseball parlance, they don't just aim for singles and doubles; they swing for the fences.

Swinging for the fences means stepping into opportunities that stretch you, challenge you, and push you to rise above doubts, both your own and others'. These are the defining moments when you're called to give your best, knowing the stakes are high but trusting that the effort will be worth it.

This requires more than just courage. It demands faith, preparation, and the wisdom to navigate resistance. There will always be voices telling you to play small, to stay safe, to avoid the discomfort that comes with taking bold action. But greatness lies in rejecting those limitations, in stepping forward with confidence, and in trusting that the unique gifts and vision you bring to the table are enough.

Whether you're leading a team, stepping into an unfamiliar role, or facing an unexpected challenge, the key is to swing for the fences—not for glory but because the effort itself has the power to transform you and those around you.

YOU WANT ME?

That said, not everyone appreciates this swing-for-the-fences mentality, and there will always be those who try to hold you back. I think back to my time at the Carver Center for Climate Justice. One day, I received an email inviting me to be the commencement speaker at Northeastern University's College of Science graduation in May 2023.

Initially, I was skeptical. My first thought was "Are you sure you want me? "At the time, I was the interim CEO, following a predecessor who had held the role for a decade. I wondered if they had reached out to me solely because my predecessor was no longer available. But they assured me they wanted *me*, so I decided to go for it.

Unfortunately, one of my direct reports, the senior vice president of marketing, was not supportive and made it clear that she didn't think it was a good use of my time. Normally, when the CEO or interim CEO does something notable, it's highlighted on LinkedIn or the organization's website. But in this case, there was no acknowledgment. It was evident that she didn't think this event was worth promoting.

Rather than second-guess myself, I decided to press forward. As it turned out, being the commencement speaker turned out to be one of the most incredible experiences of my life. The event was held in an arena filled with over a thousand graduates, their families, and faculty. I addressed students ranging from undergraduates to PhDs and sat alongside the college dean and the university president, whose own son was graduating.

Wearing the cap and gown, receiving a framed citation, and speaking to such a prestigious audience made the moment deeply meaningful. My mother-in-law messaged me, saying no one in our family had ever done something like this. It was a source of pride for all of us.

During my speech, I encouraged the graduates to think differently and to embrace their responsibility in tackling climate change. I shared examples of impactful work being done at the Carver Center and challenged them to dream big, including preparing for vacation on the moon. If I had listened to the naysayers who thought this wasn't worth my time, I would have missed this incredible opportunity. By stepping into that commencement role, I showed my children and others that a person of color can not only achieve great things but belong at the decision-making table. There is no telling what you can do if you adopt the same mentality.

LIFT OTHERS UP RATHER THAN PULL THEM DOWN

Humans sometimes have a natural tendency to sabotage each other's success. I've observed this phenomenon, particularly among leaders of color and others striving to break barriers. This isn't to say it's universal, but when you're attempting to be the first or change the narrative, there's often resistance—both external and internal.

People of color, women, and those from marginalized communities often face an unspoken expectation to "play small." For example, people of color historically negotiate salaries less often than others and are less likely to advocate for raises.[61] This conditioning can make it even harder to challenge the status quo or reach for more.

---

61 American Psychological Association, "Bargaining while Black: The Impact of Race on the Negotiation Process," November 2018, https://www.apa.org/news/press/releases/2018/11/bargaining-black.

Yet, the onus isn't just on overcoming these societal barriers. It's also about making room for others once you achieve success. When you've fought to climb that ladder, it's your duty to ensure that others don't have to struggle the same way. Leadership isn't about pulling up the ladder behind you; it's about leaving it down and extending a hand.

As leaders, we must resist the temptation to play it safe or bring others down. We can't avoid tough conversations out of fear of losing favor. Whether it's advocating for justice, challenging outdated systems, or simply pursuing opportunities others believe are out of reach, leadership requires courage. It's about standing firm even when the road is tough, because the work of truth telling and making change is worth the cost.

BE WISE AND NOT RECKLESS

There is a clear difference between swinging for the fences and being reckless. Swinging for the fences means taking a bold, calculated risk with the potential for significant payoff, while being reckless involves hasty or thoughtless actions that disregard potential consequences.

When I think about being reckless, it's about making decisions that jeopardize the stability of your family, team, or organization. For example, if a leader makes choices that threaten financial security, like committing resources without proper planning or taking actions that could harm an organization's ability to make payroll, that's reckless. Recklessness is marked by a lack of foresight and disregard for the people and systems affected by the decision.

In contrast, swinging for the fences involves bold action, but it's grounded in strategy and awareness. Jim Collins, in *Great by Choice*, introduces the concept of "firing bullets before cannonballs." While the analogy might feel dated, the principle still holds: before you make a significant investment or sweeping change, you test the waters with smaller, more manageable steps. These "bullets" let you assess the viability of your idea and minimize risks. If those small efforts prove successful, you can confidently invest more, knowing the larger risk is justified. As journalist and author Brad Stone writes,

> We all know that if you swing for the fences, you're going to strike out a lot, but you're also going to hit some home runs. The difference between baseball and business, however, is that baseball has a truncated outcome distribution. When you swing, no matter how well you connect with the ball, the most runs you can get is four. In business, every once in a while, when you step up to the plate, you can score 1,000 runs. This long-tailed distribution of returns is why it's important to be bold.[62]

Recklessness often manifests in leaders who try to make drastic changes immediately—turning the organization 180 degrees without slowing down to assess the current state or involving others in the process. Using the metaphor of steering a ship, you can't turn a massive vessel sharply without first slowing it down.

The same applies to leading change: rushing in without giving people time to adjust or without honoring their previous efforts can alienate those invested in the current system. A new leader walking in on day two, declaring "We're scrapping this and starting over," risks not only losing credibility but also creating unnecessary resistance.

For example, whenever I am assigned to a new church, I use the first year as an opportunity to assess the strengths and growth opportunities of the leaders, members, ministers, organizations, and

---

62 Brad Stone, *Amazon Unbound: Jeff Bezos and the Invention of a Global Empire* (New York: Simon & Schuster, 2021).

ministries. I listen to member concerns, watch interpersonal interactions, observe community needs, and ask God for discernment into whether what I am hearing is rooted in a sincere desire to make a difference in the lives of others or to settle scores and maintain power.

Invariably, I am told that a certain member is problematic or that another should no longer hold a leadership position. I have found that people's true colors will shine through in time. If a person overpromises and underdelivers, or if another rises to a challenge when given an opportunity to step up, those traits will rise to the surface too. And in the words of Dr. Maya Angelou, "When someone shows you who they are, believe them."

Recklessness, in this case, would be steamrolling ahead with other people's plans for the church, dismissing musicians, and reshaping the congregation in their image. Swinging for the fences, however, means making bold decisions that best support the mission of the church by doing so thoughtfully and in a way that builds consensus over time.

The key difference lies in approach. Recklessness ignores the voices, values, and efforts of everyone, prioritizing speed or ambition over stability. Swinging for the fences, while ambitious, respects the existing structure and considers how to align bold actions with the broader goals and well-being of those impacted. It's about moving forward with courage but also with wisdom.

DO WHAT YOU CAN, BUT DON'T DO IT ALL

Swinging for the fences doesn't mean the entire weight of a church or organization rests on your shoulders. Leadership is not about being a savior. Whether you're a pastor, an executive, or a community leader, your role is to steward resources, share a vision, and build systems that outlast your tenure.

One of the greatest mistakes leaders make is believing they alone are the solution to every problem. It's tempting to think, "I have the skills, the vision, and the drive to fix this," but the reality is that no single leader can bear the weight of a struggling organization or church on their shoulders. Success, when it happens, is rarely the result of one person's efforts—it's a culmination of contributions from many, often over time. Similarly, challenges are usually rooted in long-standing issues that require collective action to address.

This dynamic is especially challenging for pastors. Congregations often adopt a savior mentality, expecting the next leader to fix everything. But systemic problems like mismanagement, poor stewardship, or cultural stagnation go far deeper than anyone can resolve. The same holds true in other organizations. Leaders who try to act as saviors rather than as stewards often carry burdens they were never meant to bear.

In the movie *Waiting for Superman*, Dr. Geoffrey Canada, founder of the Harlem Children's Zone, highlights the importance of taking action while rejecting the savior complex. Faced with deeply rooted systemic issues in education, he didn't wait for someone else to step in. Instead, he built a community-driven model that addressed education, healthcare, and social services together. Importantly, Canada didn't assume he could do it all himself. He built a strong team and empowered others, showing that leadership is about collaboration and shared responsibility.

This perspective doesn't negate the sacrifice leadership demands. Sacrificial giving is part of faith and service, but it must be done wisely. You cannot give so much of yourself—financially, emotionally, spiritually, or physically—that you undermine your ability to lead effectively. Whether in a ministry or a corporate setting, it's crucial to invest your resources strategically and to establish boundaries.

Too often, leaders neglect their own long-term health and well-being in the name of their calling. I've seen pastors pour everything into their congregations, only for their families to face financial hardship when the pastors are no longer in ministry. Trusting in God's provision is important but so is taking proactive steps to protect yourself and your family.

Leadership isn't about doing it all yourself; it's about empowering others and fostering a shared commitment to the mission. Swinging for the fences doesn't mean doing everything yourself or taking reckless risks. It means stepping into your role with courage, faith, and wisdom, ready to give your best effort even when outcomes aren't guaranteed.

You can't do it all, but you can do more than you think!

REMEMBER: SWING FOR THE FENCES

Starting off this book, I noted in the introduction that many naturally see this large disconnect between being a pastor and being a CEO. But the truth is, the best lives are those where everything is integrated. Sure, maybe you're not a pastor or leader of a company, but your faith informs the way you work, and your discipline of hard work helps strengthen your faith.

Ephesians 2:20 says that Christ is to be the cornerstone of a Christian's faith. A cornerstone is not added last; it's laid first, and everything else is built around it. It's a foundation, not an afterthought.

In the same way, your faith is not something to tack on after achieving success. It is the foundation on which everything else is built. Your corporate achievements, your professional acumen, your leadership—all these are shaped and supported by that cornerstone. Without it, none of these other things would be possible.

Too often, we compartmentalize our faith and our professional lives as though the two are incompatible, but that's a false divide. The same God who has shaped your values, your faith, and your character has also equipped you with the skills and expertise you use in your career. These things are not separate; they are intertwined, and they reflect the wholeness of who you are.

But because of Christ, you have everything you need and can be who he has designed you to be. The message I want to leave you with is this: *Who are you not to shine?* Who are you to believe that your gifts and talents—gifts given to you by God—aren't meant to be fully utilized in all areas of your life?

So as you close this book, I encourage you to reflect on how you can live a life of integration—where your faith and your work, your personal values and your professional ambitions, come together to reflect the fullness of who God has called you to be.

Every step you take, every decision you make, is an opportunity to build on the cornerstone of Christ, trusting that he has equipped you with everything you need to succeed. Don't hold back or shrink from the light within you. Step boldly into the spaces where your gifts are needed, knowing that you are fulfilling a purpose far greater than yourself. Shine brightly, not just for your own success, but for the impact you can have on the world around you.

BULLETIN NOTES

FOUR KEY TAKEAWAYS:

- ☑ Bold leadership requires taking calculated risks, stepping beyond your comfort zone, and acting with courage and faith—transforming both yourself and those around you.
- ☑ The best lives are those where faith and work are integrated, reflecting a seamless alignment of values, ambitions, and purpose.
- ☑ True leadership is about stewardship, empowering others, and building sustainable systems, not carrying the weight of an organization alone.
- ☑ Your unique gifts and talents are meant to be fully utilized; embrace them unapologetically and trust that God has equipped you for the purpose he has called you to fulfill.

THREE KEY QUESTIONS:

1. In what ways are you holding yourself back from fully utilizing the gifts and opportunities God has given you?
2. How can you ensure your bold actions are grounded in wisdom and preparation rather than recklessness?
3. What steps can you take to integrate your faith and professional life more fully so that both reflect the wholeness of who you are?

CONCLUSION

Leadership, like life, is about preparation, adaptability, and courage. Throughout these pages, we've explored tools, lessons, and examples designed to help you navigate the challenges and opportunities that come your way. Think of these lessons not as a rigid formula but as plays in your leadership playbook—strategies that might not come into play every day but will prove invaluable when the right moment arises.

Just as a football coach doesn't call every play in each game, you won't use every lesson immediately. But having them in your arsenal means you'll be ready to rise to the occasion when it matters most. The same applies to this book. You may not need the ideas here on day one or even day fifteen, but there will come a time when the wisdom within these pages resonates deeply and guides you toward success.

This book isn't meant to be read once and shelved. It's a resource to revisit, a guide to consult as you encounter new situations and challenges. The questions at the end of each chapter are there to prompt reflection, foster growth, and help you prepare for those defining moments when the right decision can make all the difference.

Leadership isn't about always knowing exactly what to do. It's about being ready to respond when the unexpected happens. It's about having the courage to step forward, the humility to keep learning, and the wisdom to draw from the tools and lessons you've gathered along the way. My hope is that this book becomes a trusted companion on your journey, offering insight, encouragement, and inspiration as you navigate the complexities of leadership and life.

As you close these pages, take with you the confidence to shine, the courage to take calculated risks, and the understanding that every moment of preparation equips you for greatness. And remember, the play you've never run before might just be the one that leads you to victory when you need it most. Keep this playbook close, and let it guide you as you lead with purpose, integrity, and faith.

ABOUT THE AUTHOR

Rev. Kevin T. Taylor is an ordained minister in the African Methodist Episcopal Church. In his career in for-profit and not-for-profit businesses, he has managed budgets of $180M+ and served as COO, CFO, and CEO of organizations in the education and clean energy sectors. He is a sought-out preacher, teacher, workshop presenter, event planner, social justice advocate, and author of newspaper articles and op-eds in numerous regional and national publications. Influenced by luminaries such as Bishop Richard Allen and Booker T. Washington and the ministries of Revs. Howard Thurman, Dr. Martin Luther King Jr., and Racquel S. Lettsome, PhD, Rev. Taylor is a native of Ann Arbor, Michigan, and now lives in New England with his family.

www.ingramcontent.com/pod-product-compliance
Lightning Source LLC
LaVergne TN
LVHW091546040926
847245LV00002B/13
9798891880078